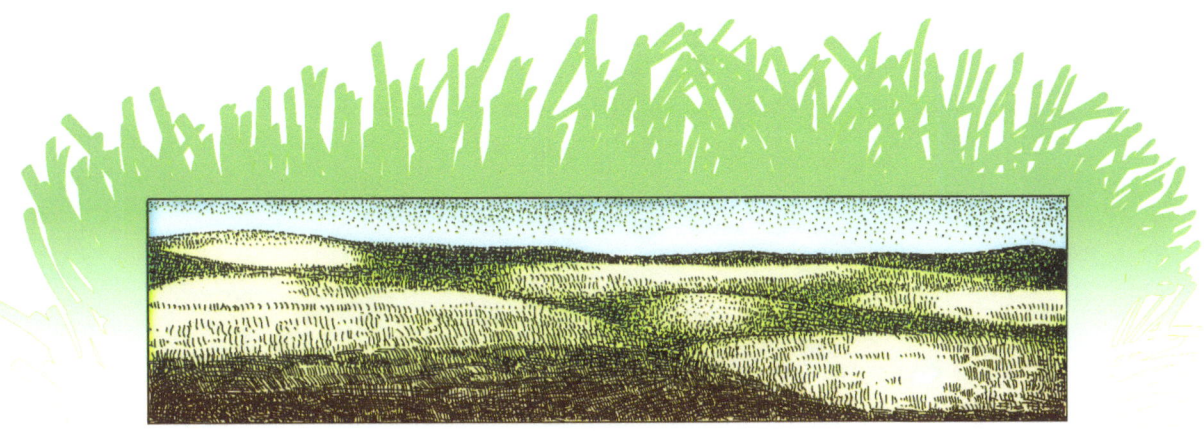

Arc of Grass

Glen Smith

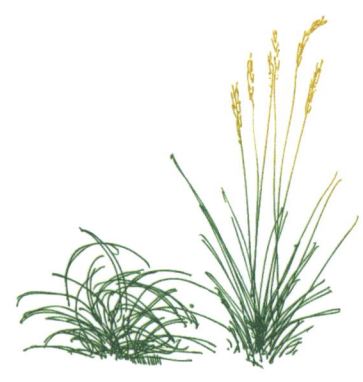

My thanks to Rosella Goodwill, Oliver Archdale,
Leslie Fourstar and to the people of Wolf Point, Poplar,
and Glasgow, Montana, for wonderful memories.

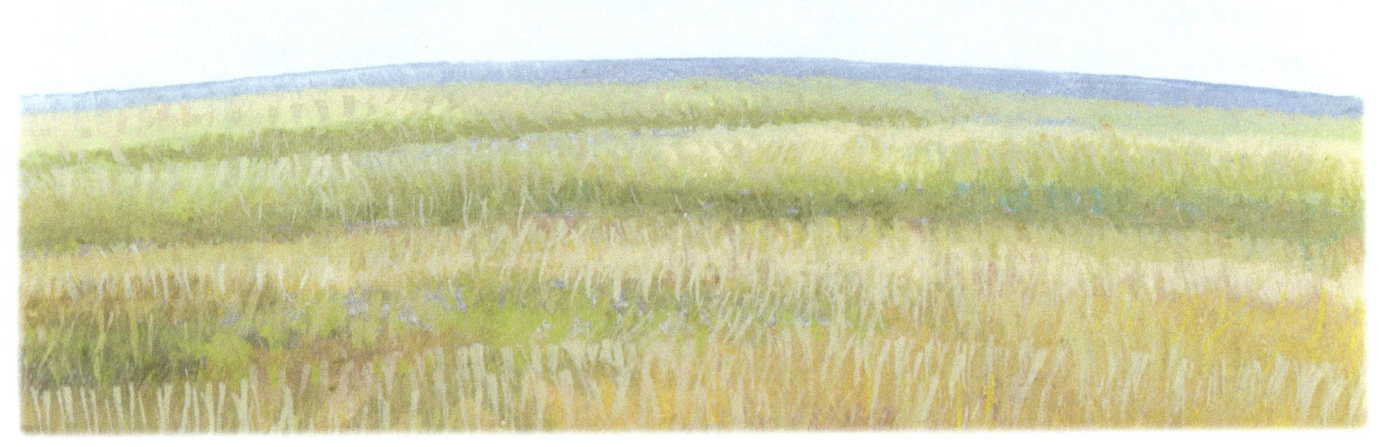

Arc of Grass

Looking north from the top of Big Spring's **Scenic Mountain** one can see the vast arc of the Earth. Contained are our grassy plains, which stretch beyond our vision. Each blade of grass springs from the in common DNA of the prairie earth. Its horizontal layers of color unfold beneath mobile skies. In Texas, the Comanche, and on the northern plains, the Assiniboine and Sioux roamed freely. Today cattle feed on grass eaten by past buffalo. Lubbock cotton and Montana wheat replace natural grasses. Towns create hubs between rail and roads crossing the prairie. Giant wind turbines newly rise. Yet these turning turbine forests seem as blades of grass within our Earth's arc.

      Our Great Plains still abides.

Heritage Museum of Big Spring, Texas

This vision quest is presented in three parts. First, every memory of the past was initially experienced in the present. Secondly, when we remember personal events of the past we must connect those memories in time and space to the world that was outside our personhood. Thus, understanding. Yet thirdly, flashed images of our past intrude on our present NOW. Thus, feeling.

Glen Smith

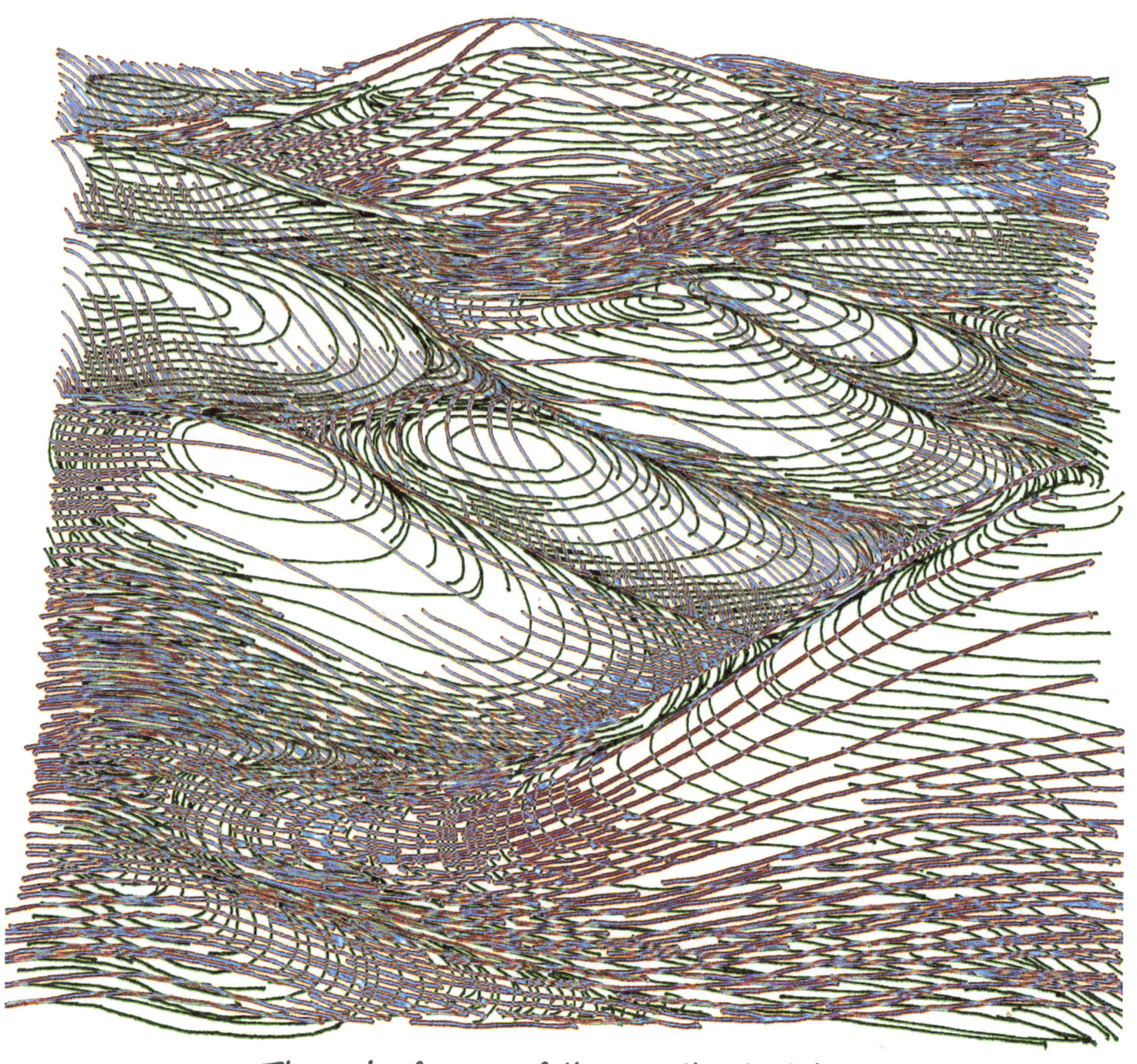

The wireframe of the earth stretches
the skin of the Great Plains.

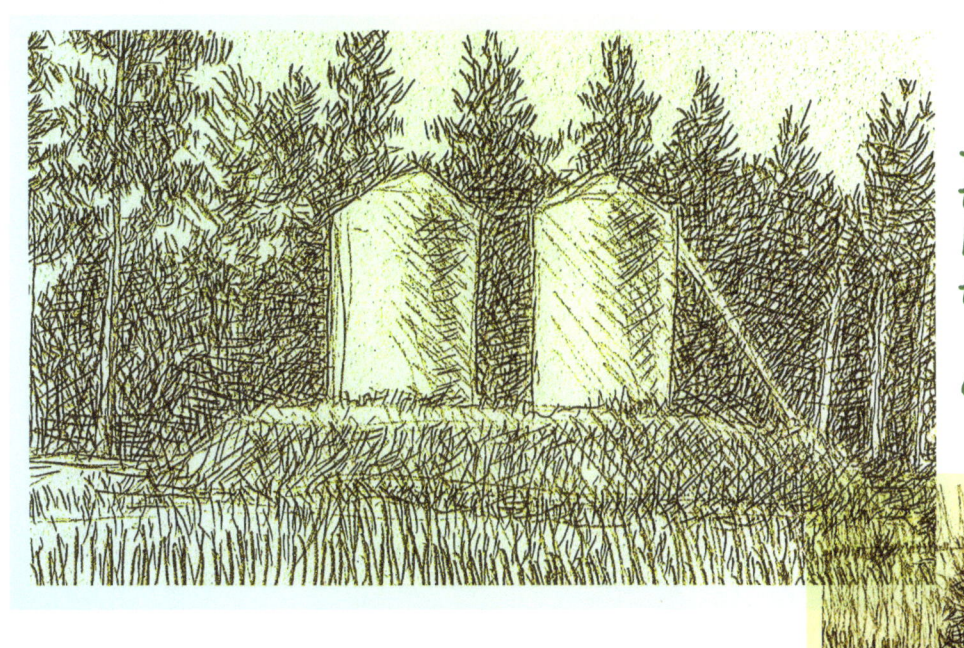

Journey from
the pine and
hardwoods
to savanna

Grass springs forth.

Protecting the earth
like soft hairs protect a
mother's newborn

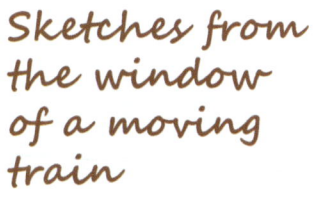

Sketches from
the window
of a moving
train

The flash of a
remembered
NOW

1

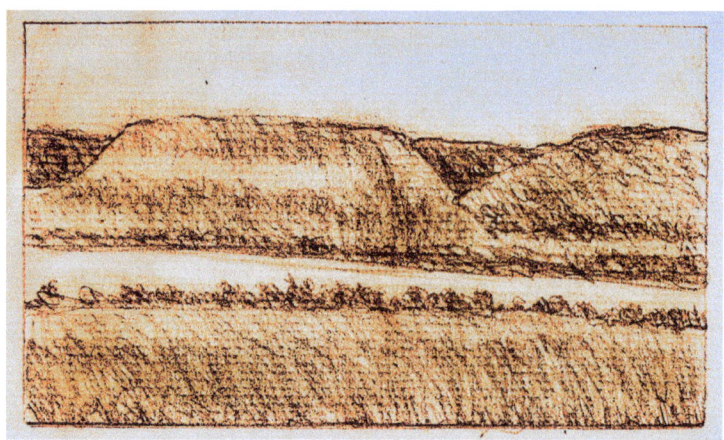
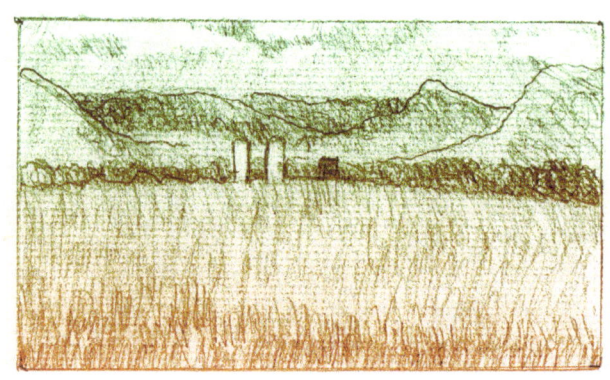
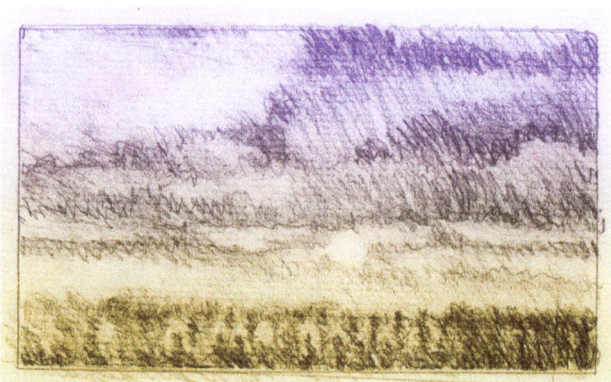

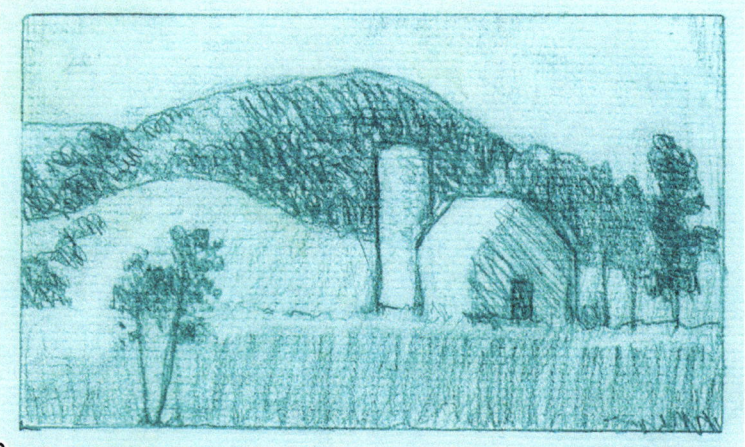
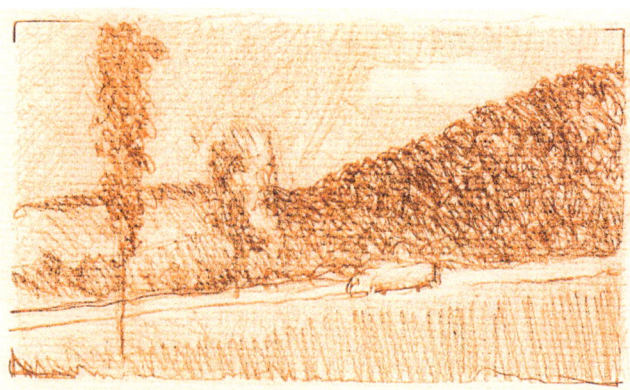

2

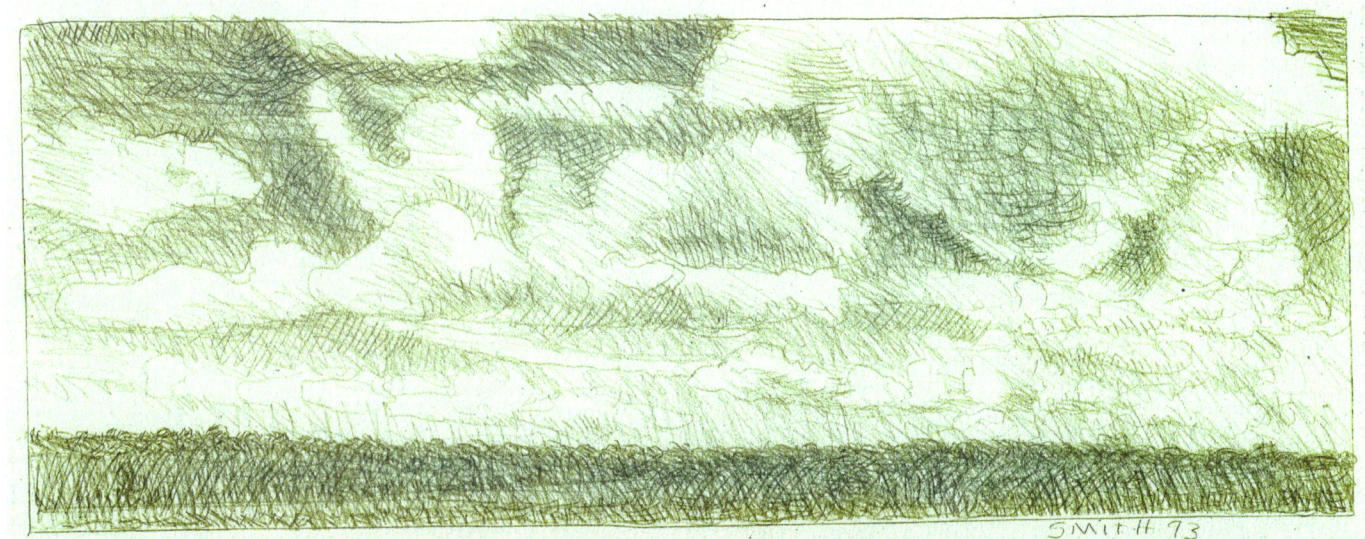

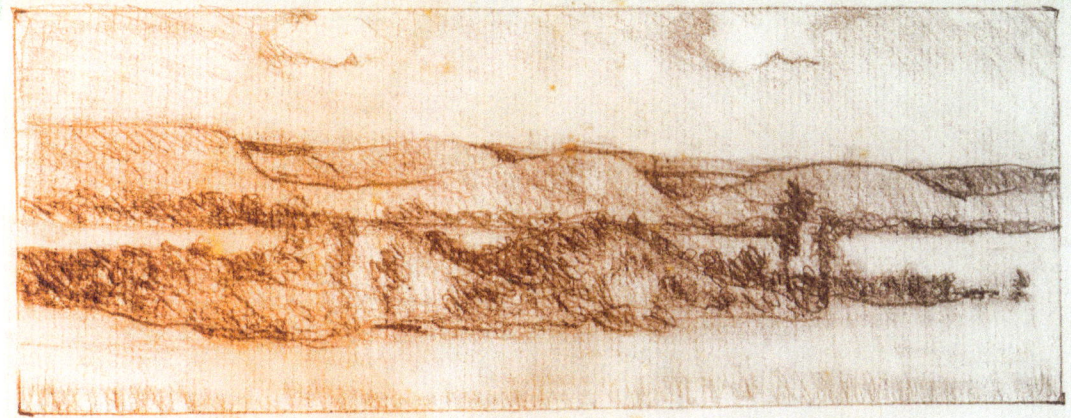

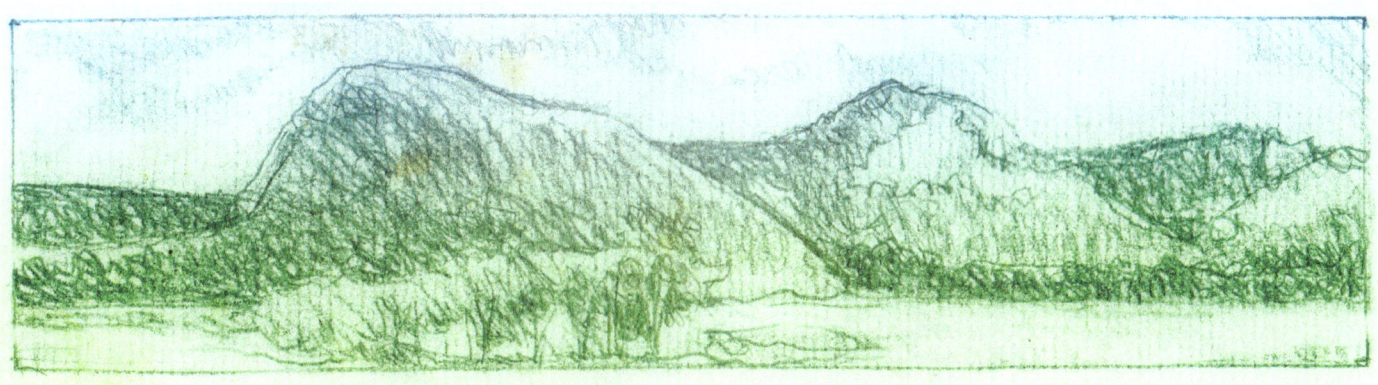

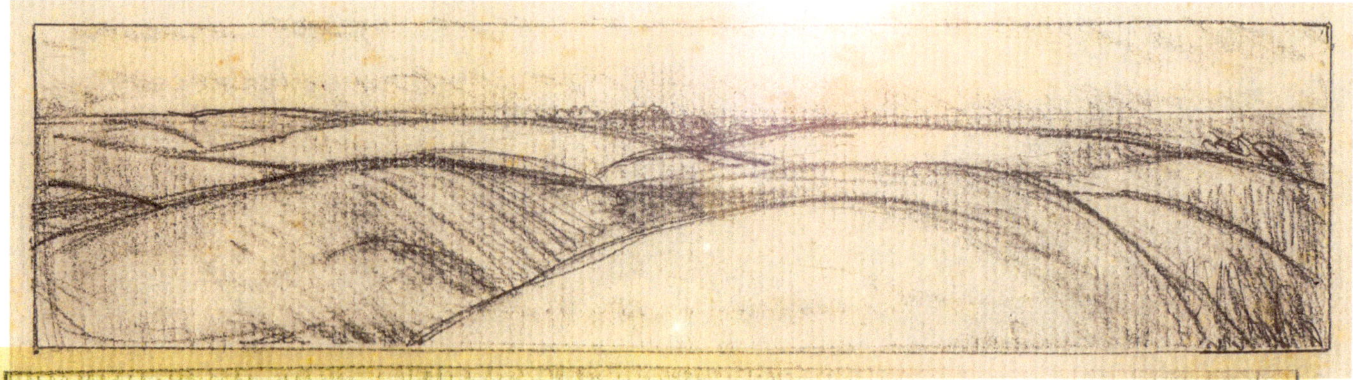

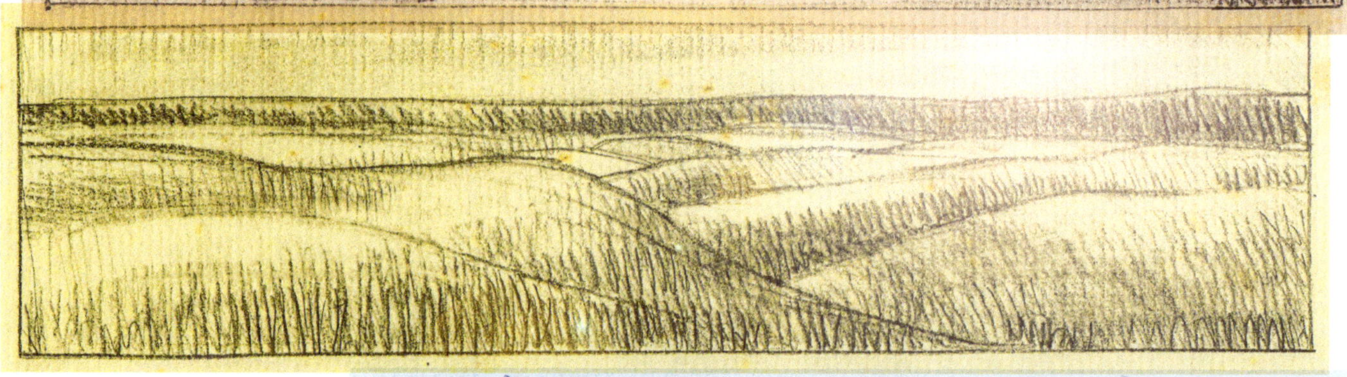

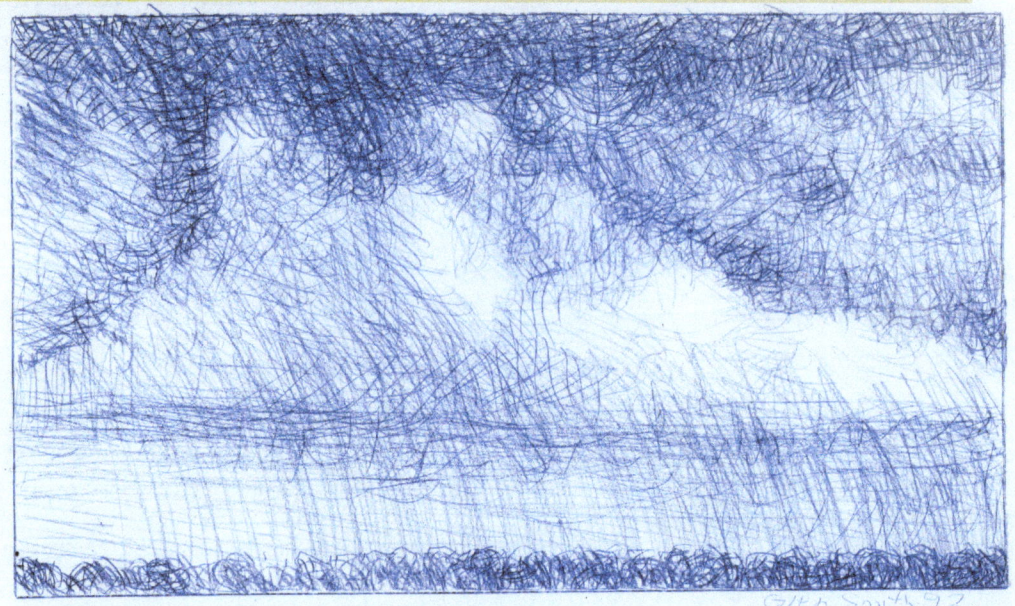

Across the
tall grass
praires the
earth bends.

4

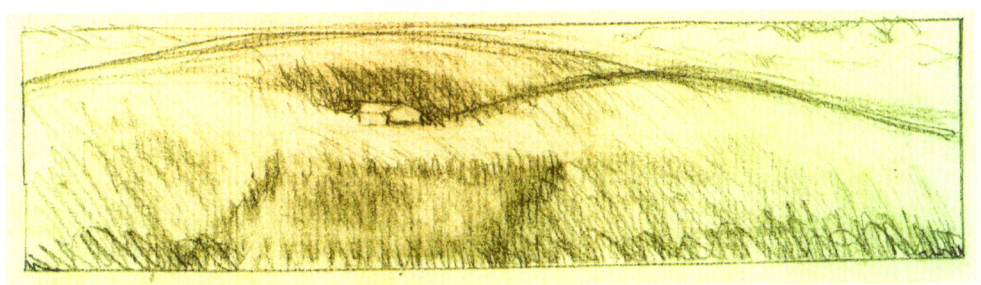

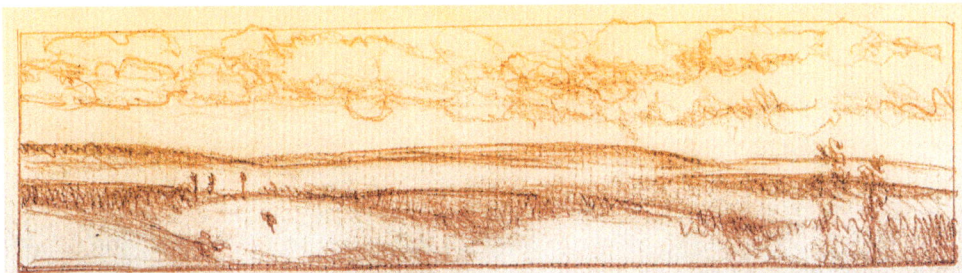

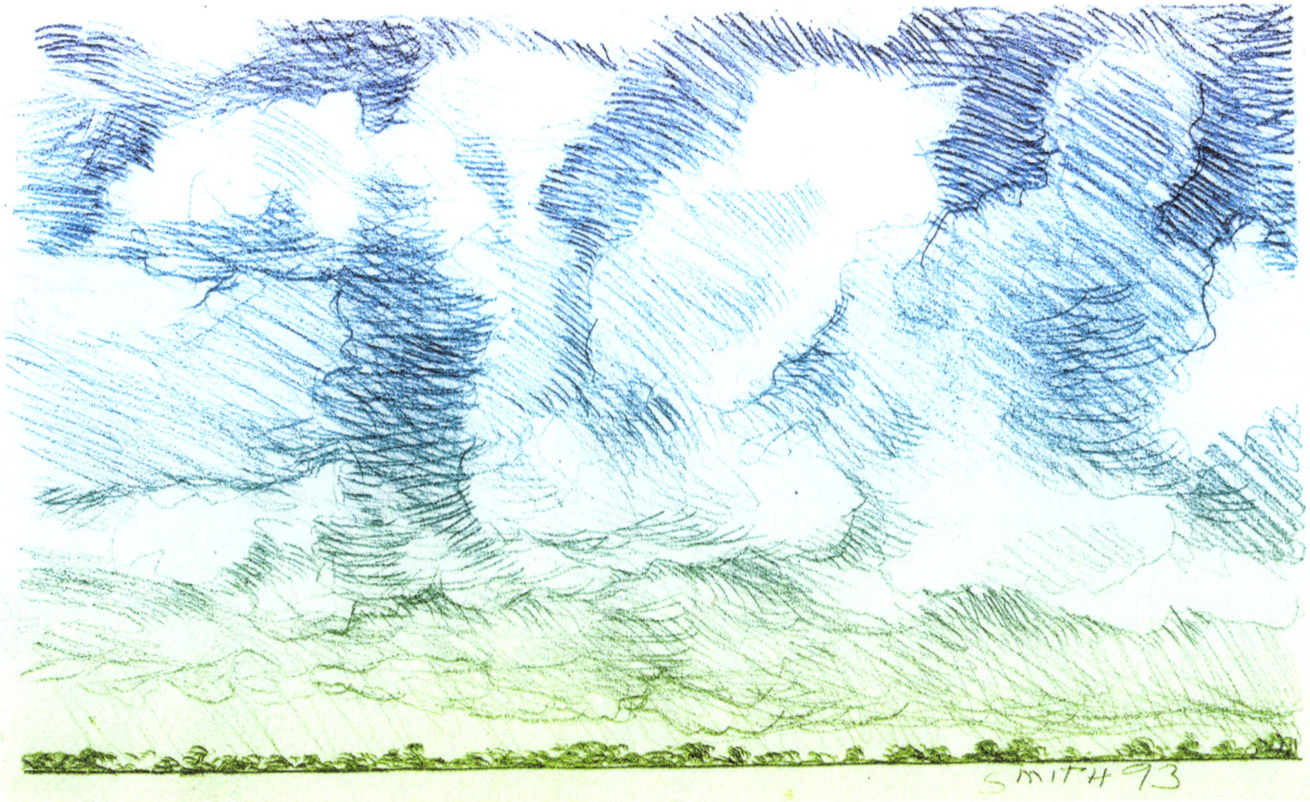

SMITH 93

5

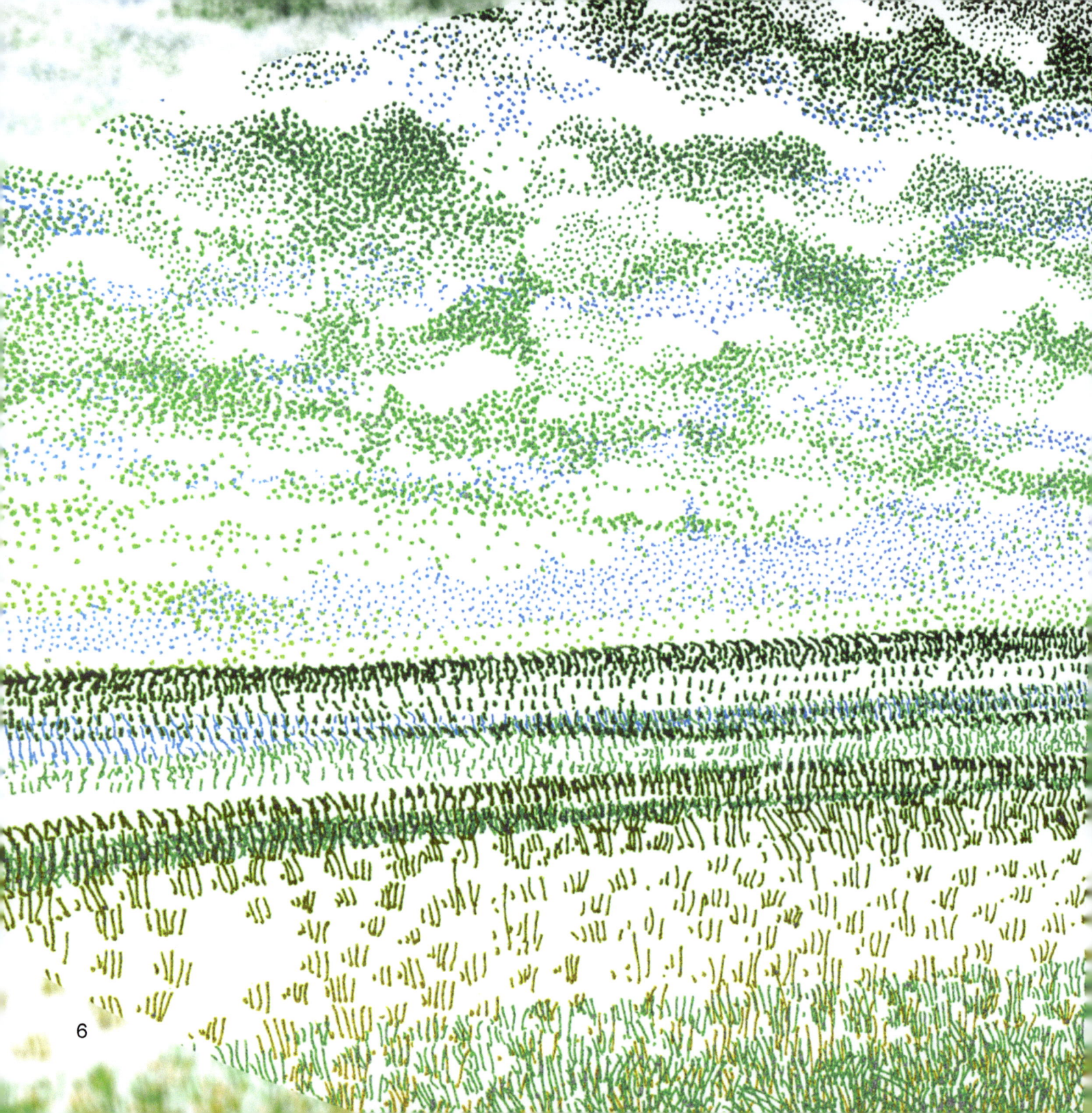

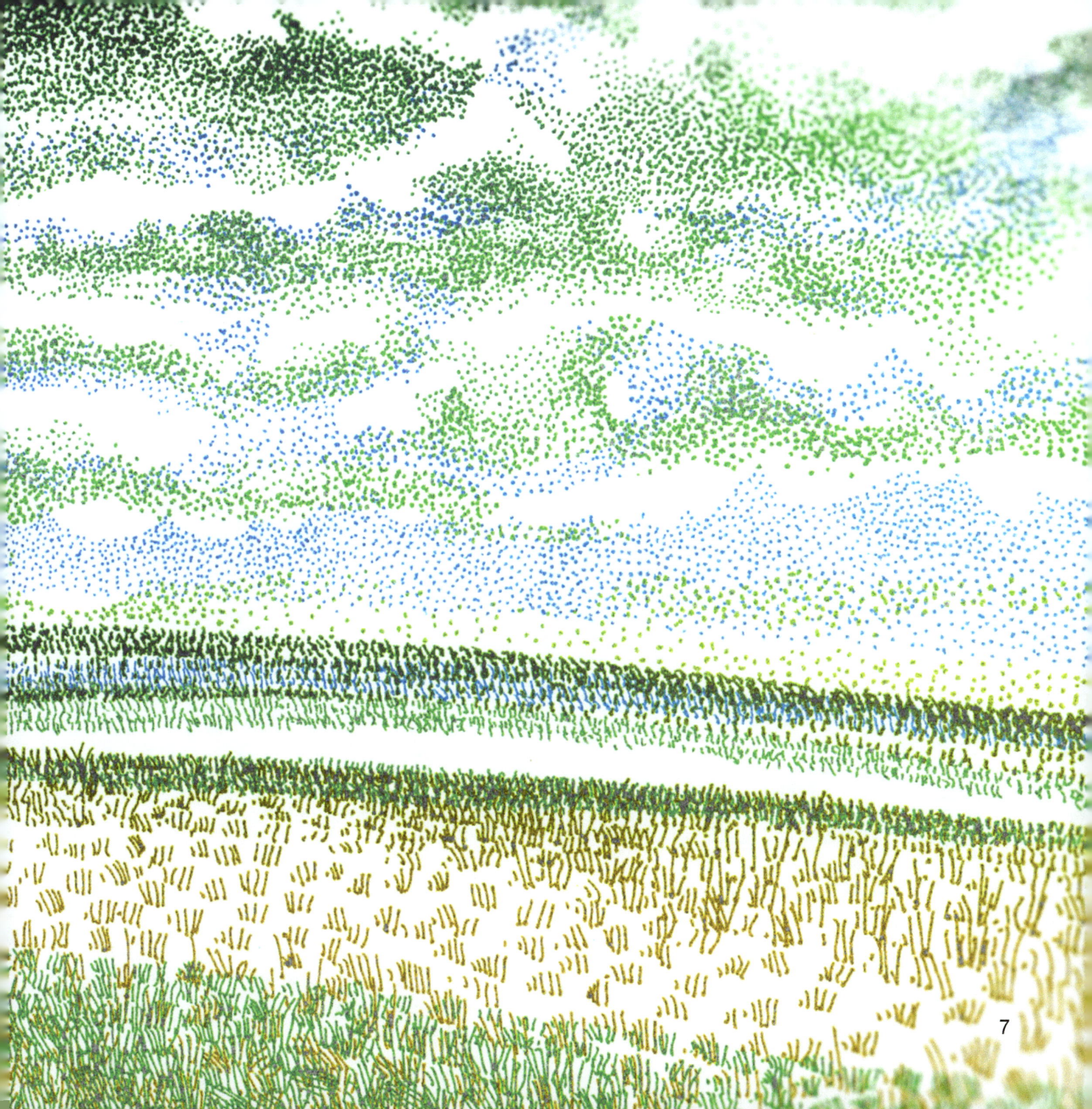

7

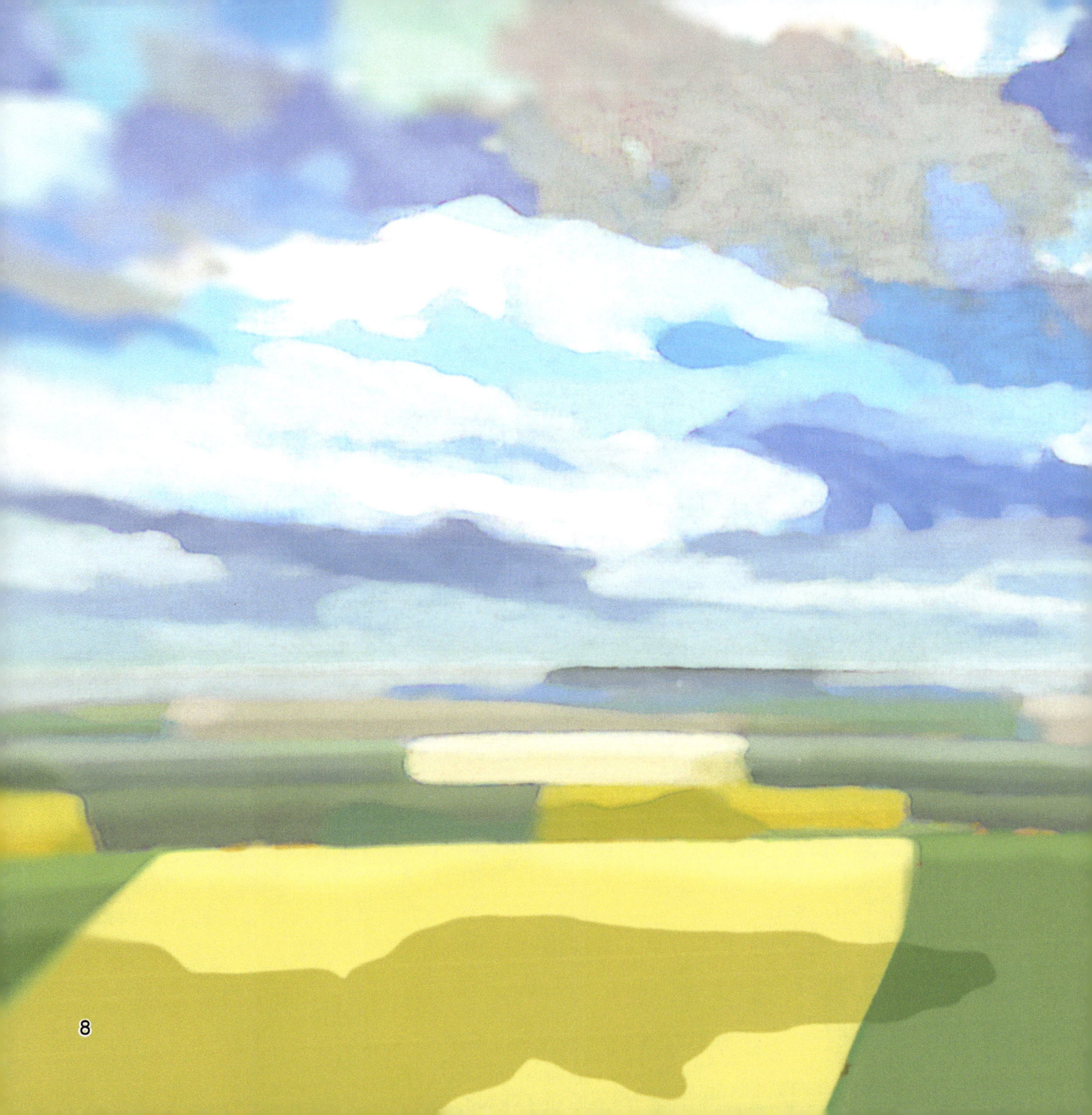

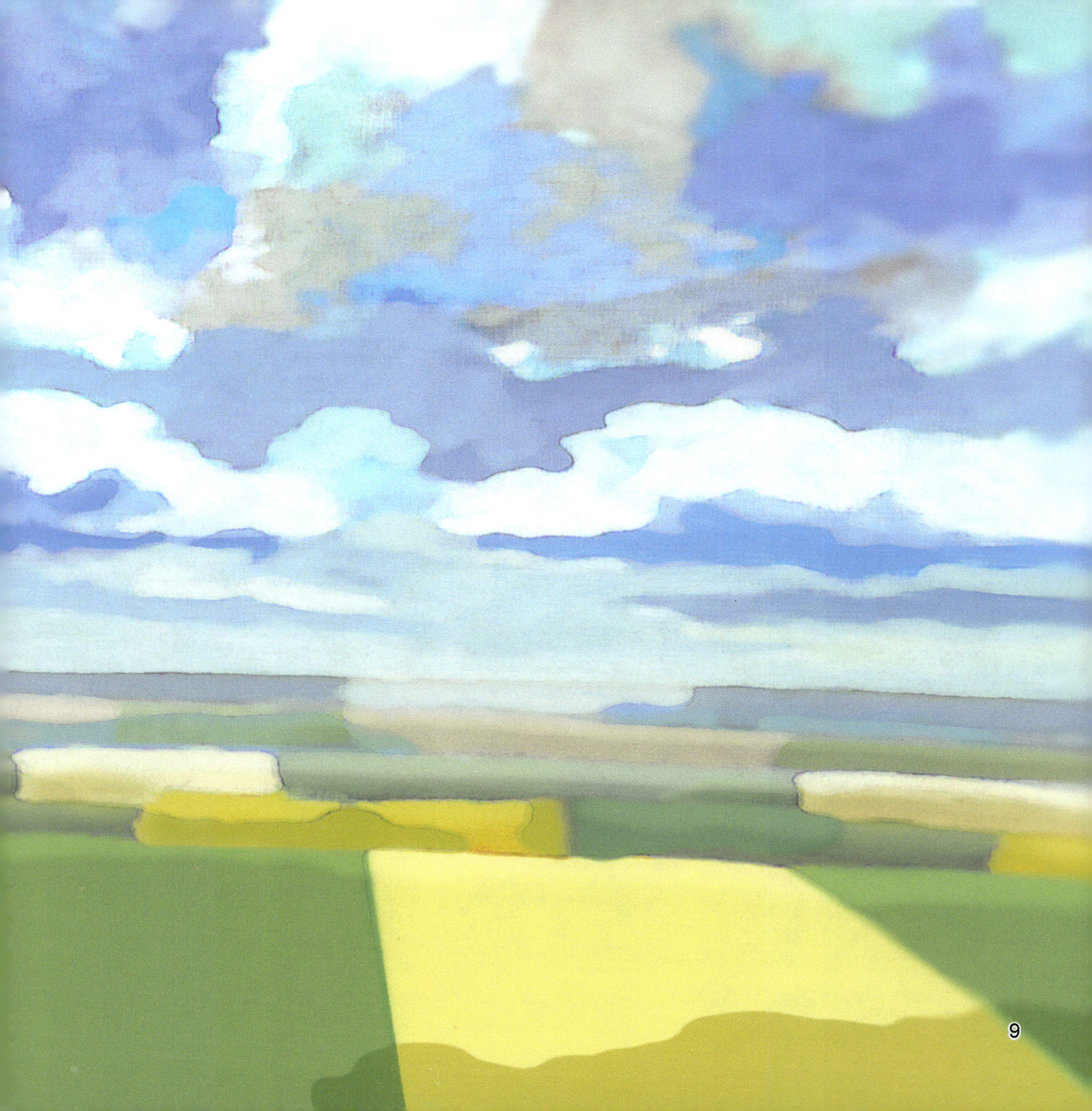

9

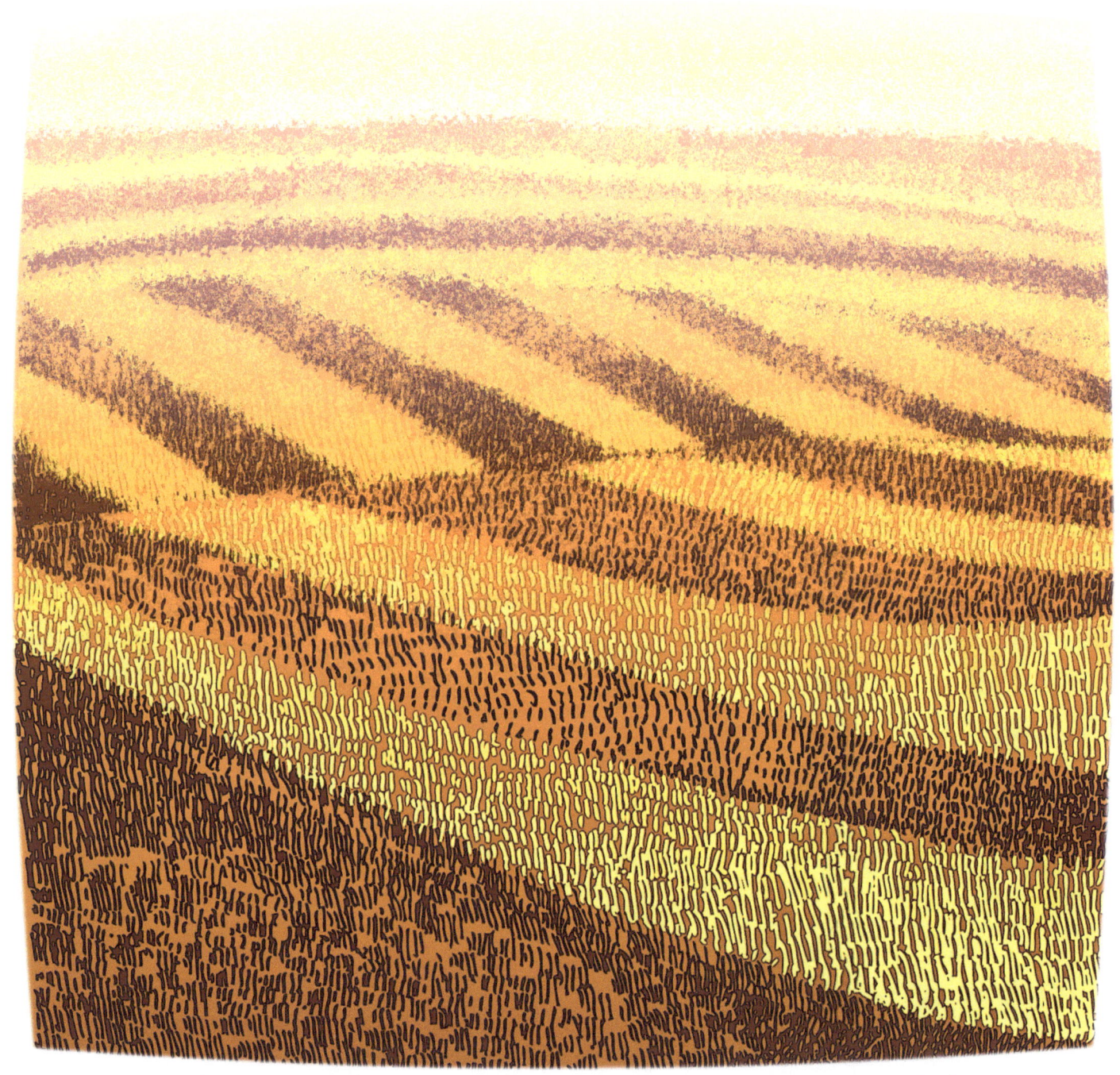

Wheat, Montana's magic carpet of gold

11

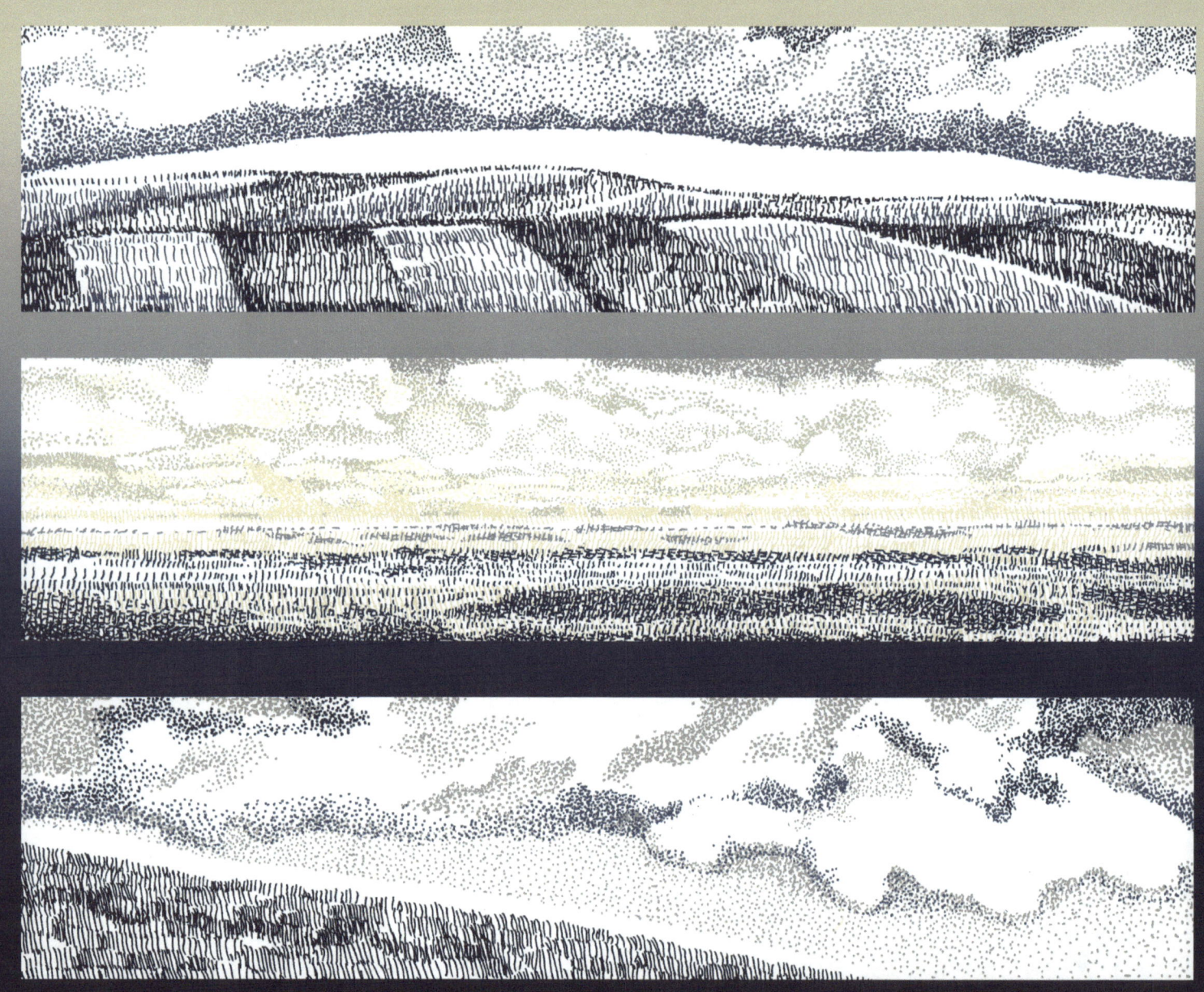

Between the sky carpet and the rolling grass we live.

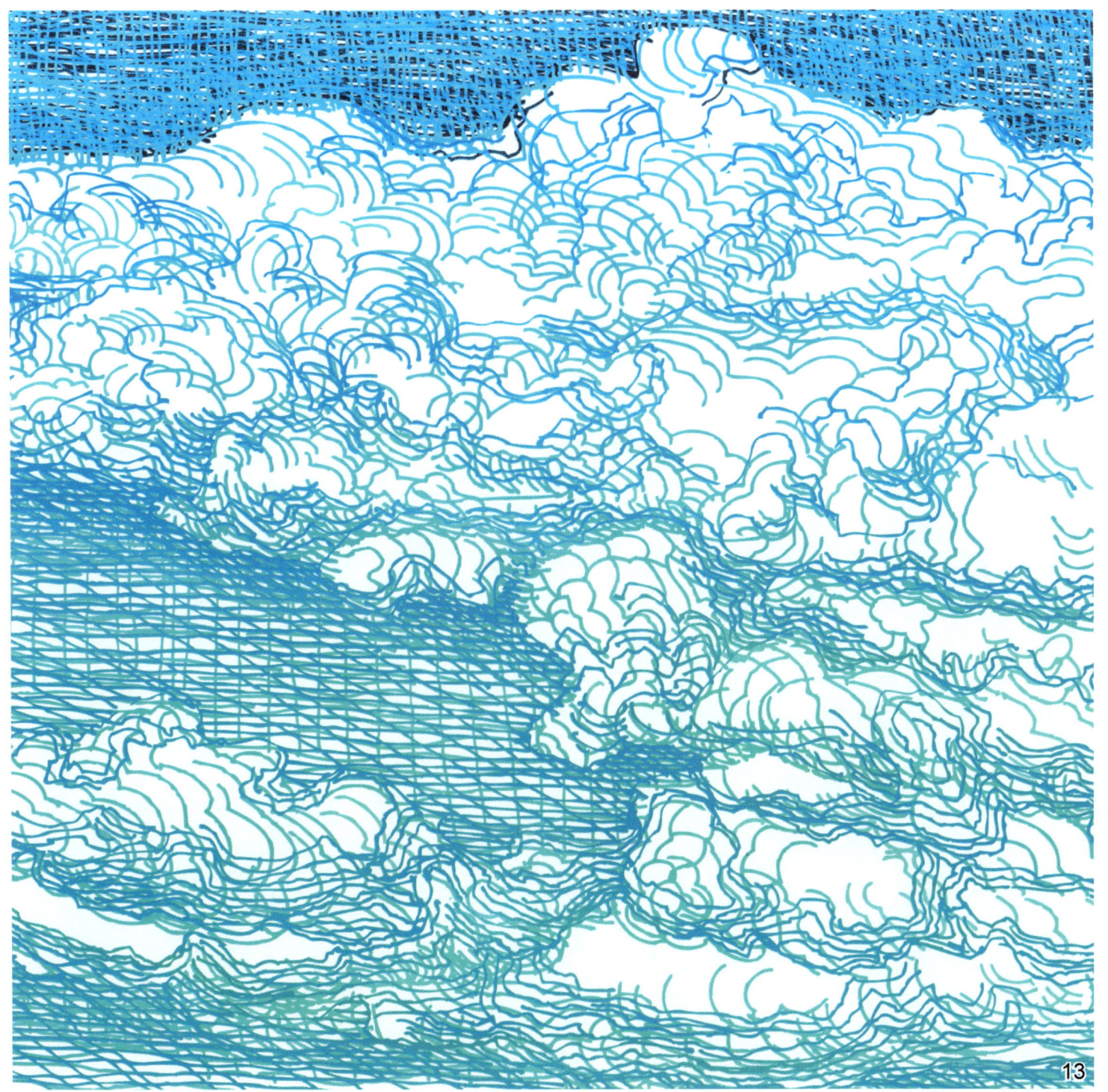

13

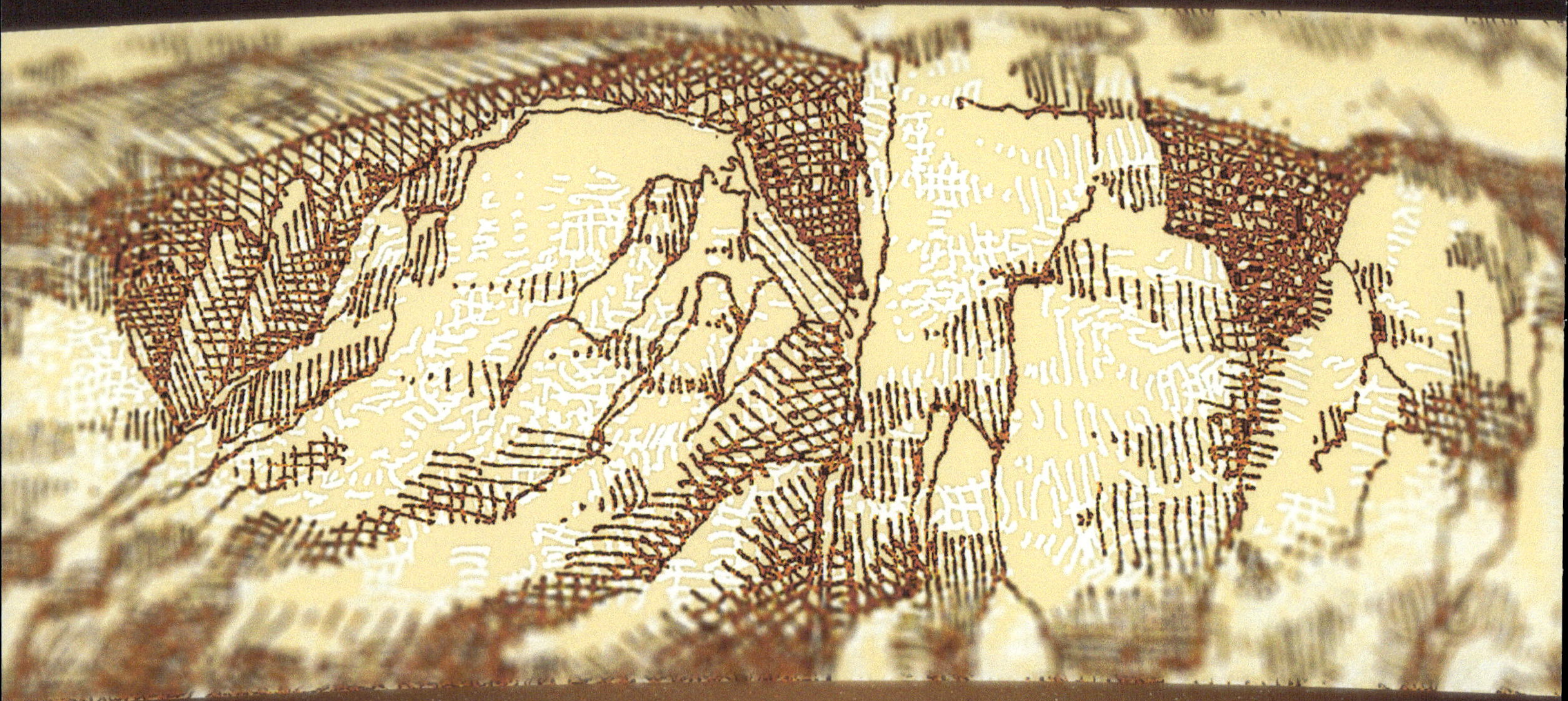

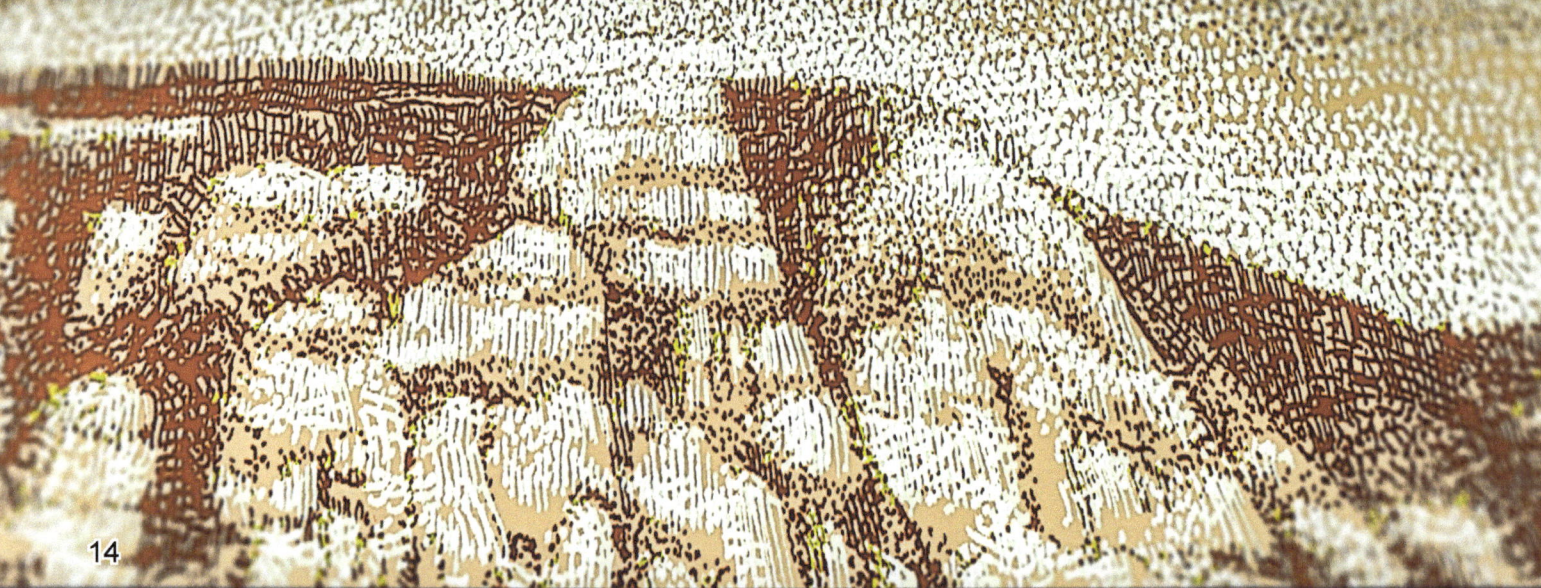

Air caverns give way to cracks in the earth.

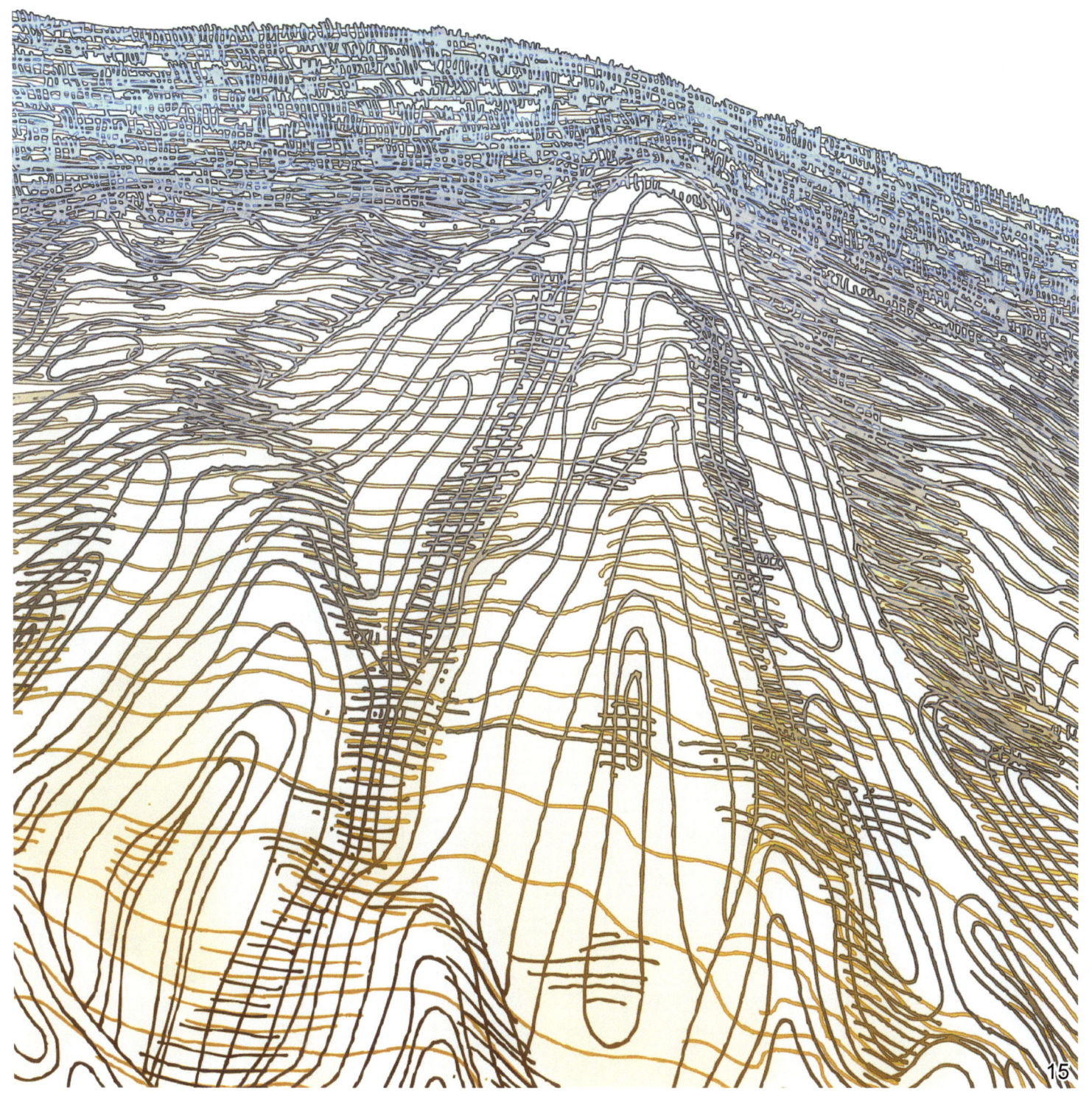

15

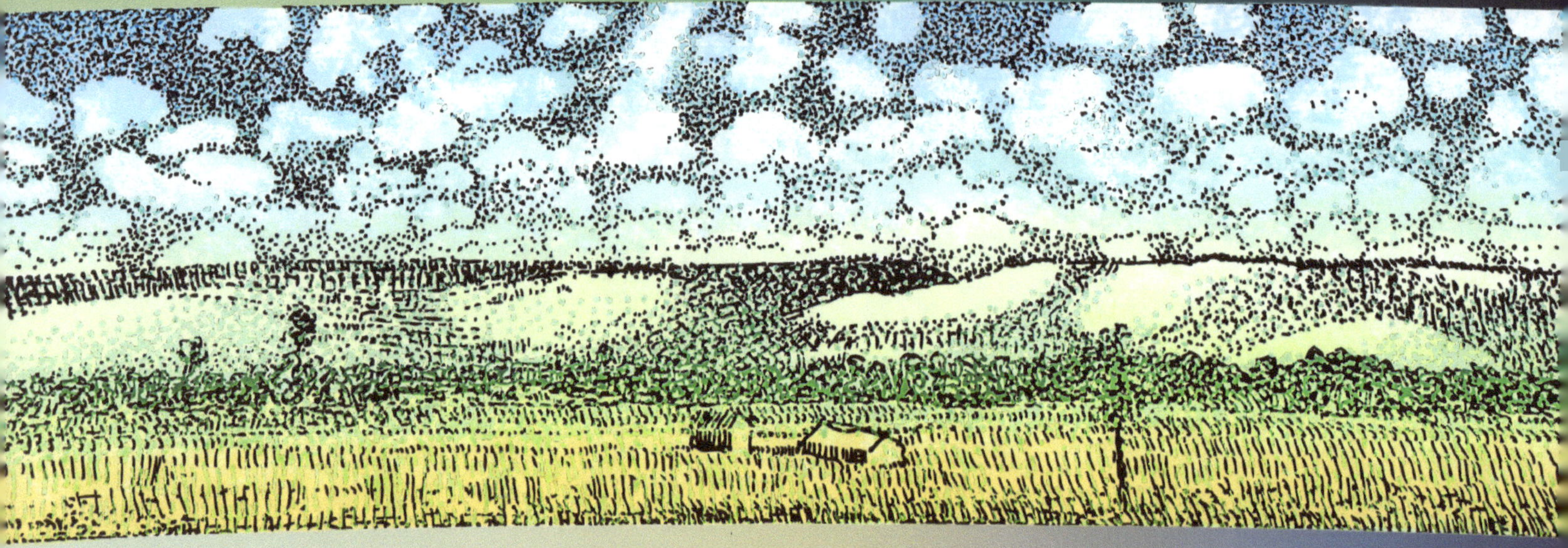

River water feeds wheat seed for man's seed.

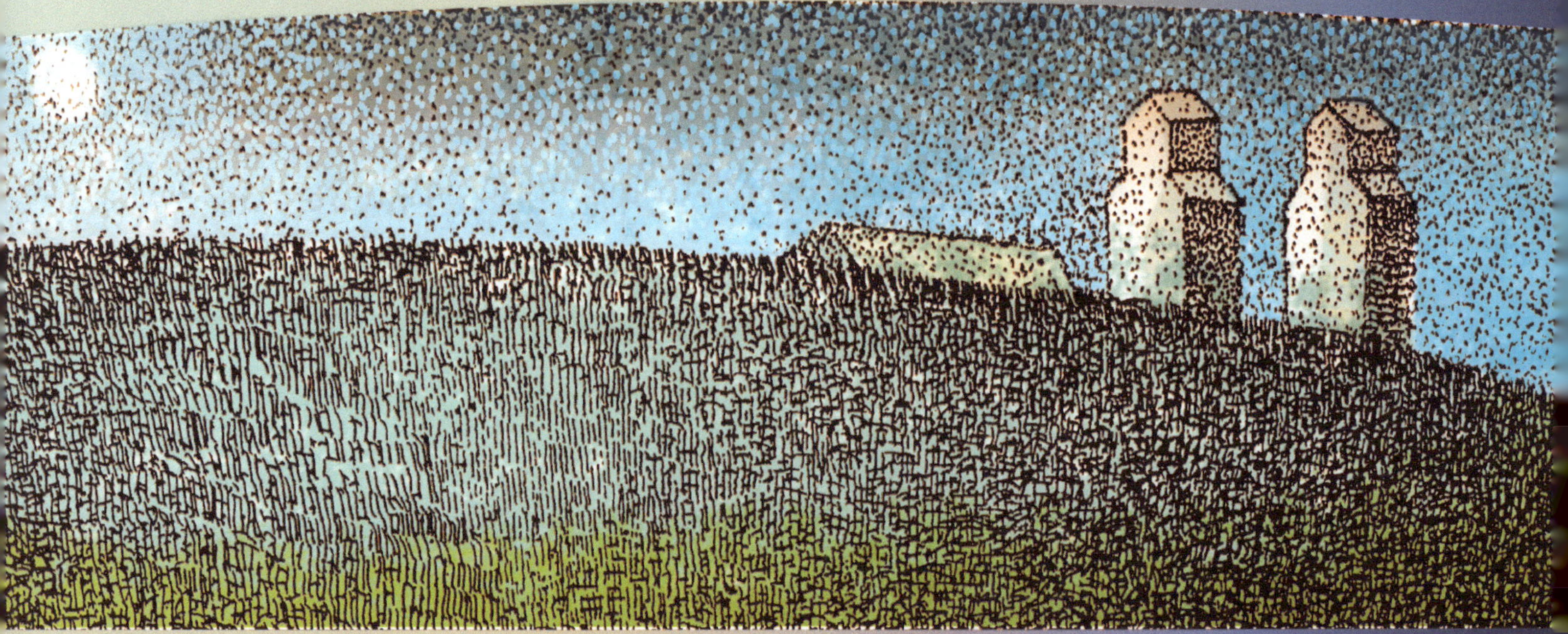

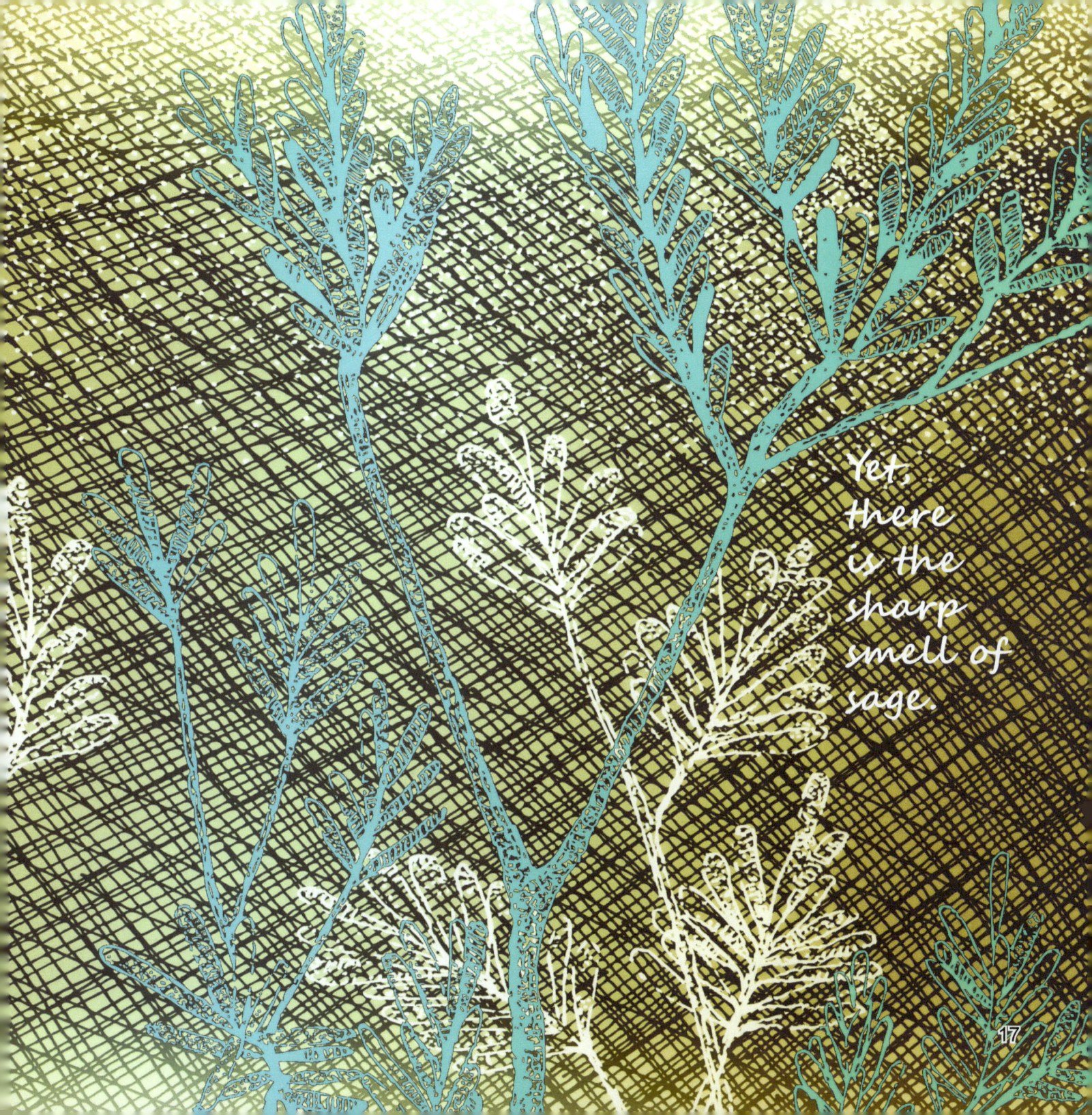

Yet, there is the sharp smell of sage.

17

Clear blue green water meets Wolf Point.

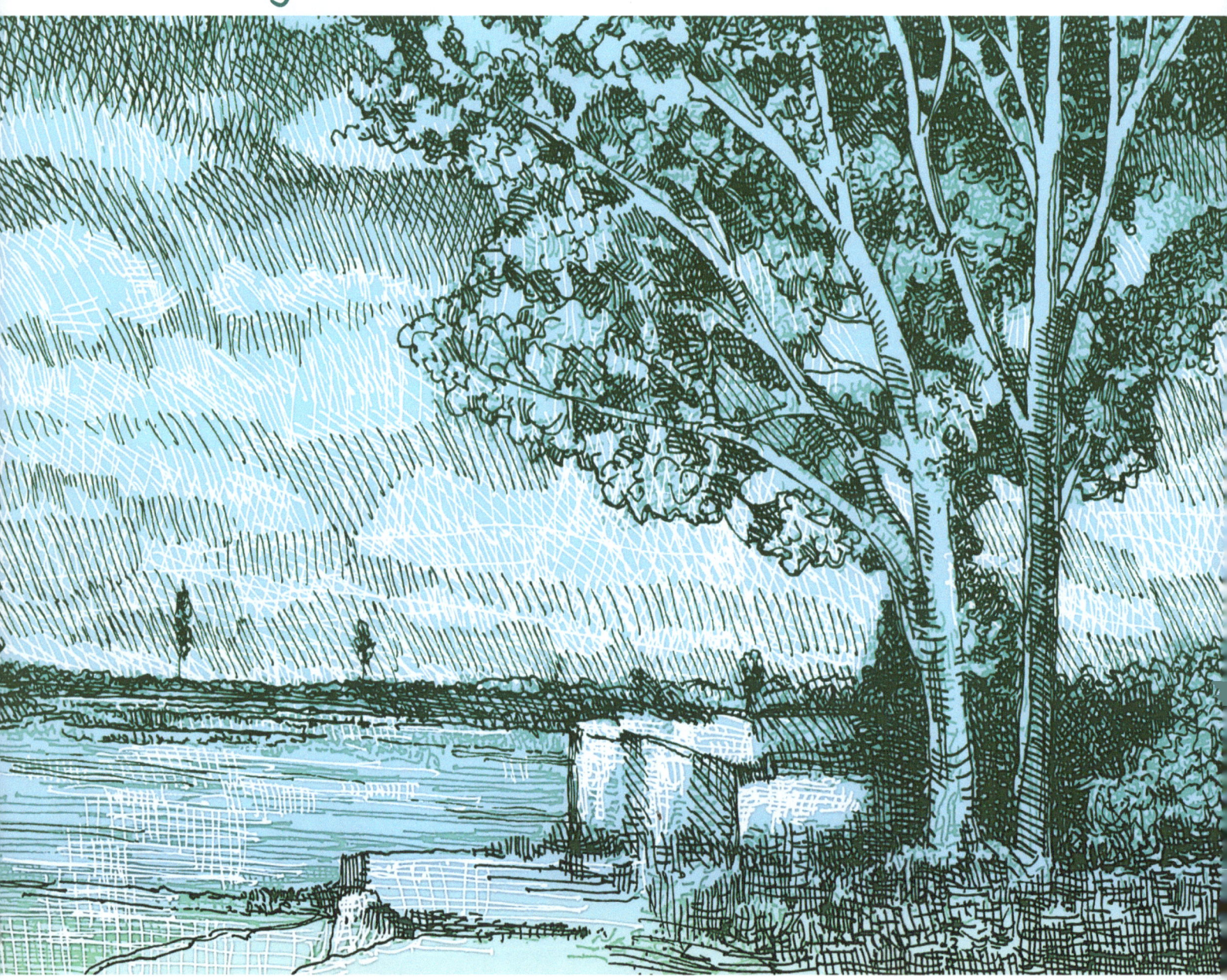

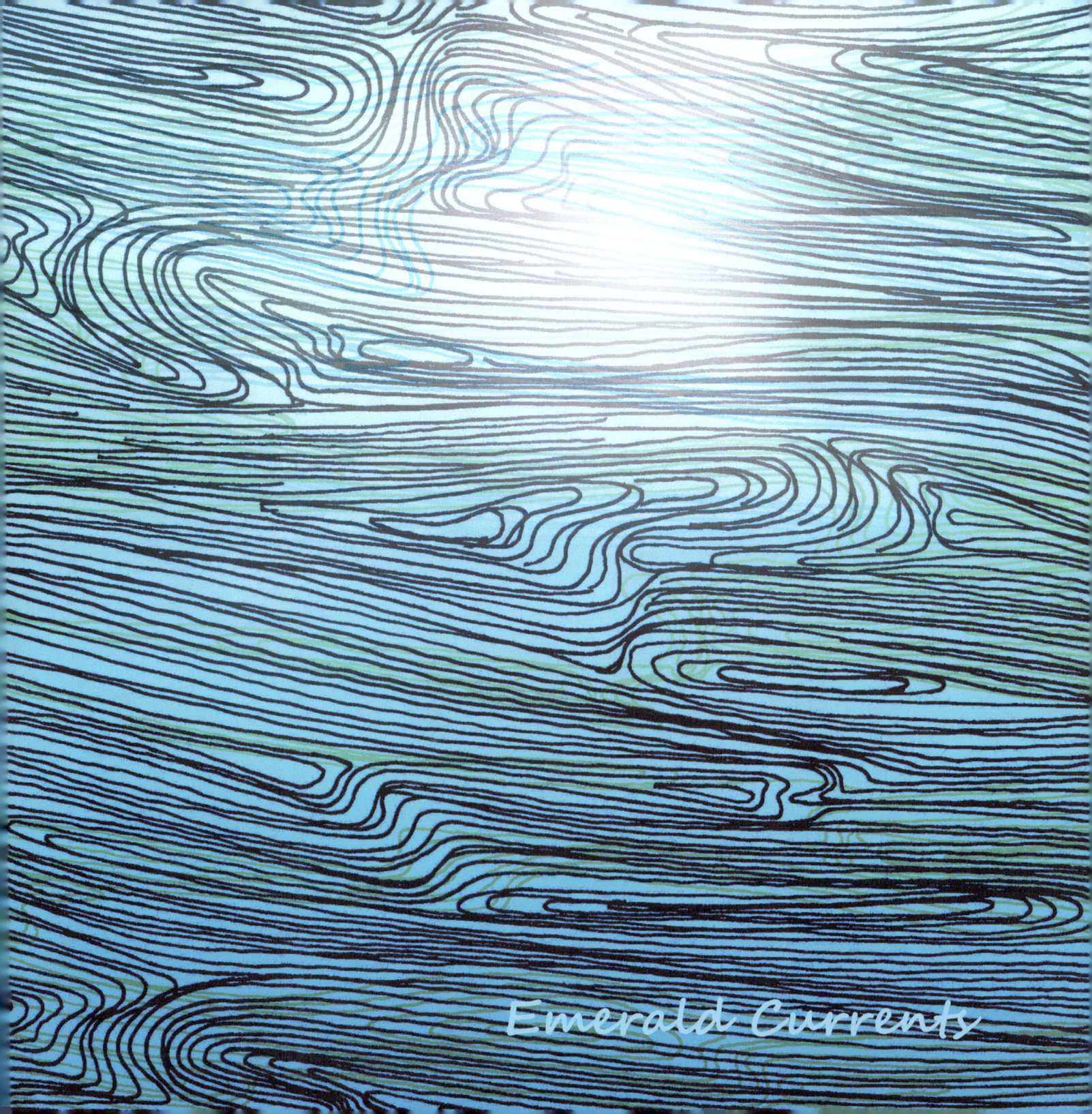

Emerald Currents

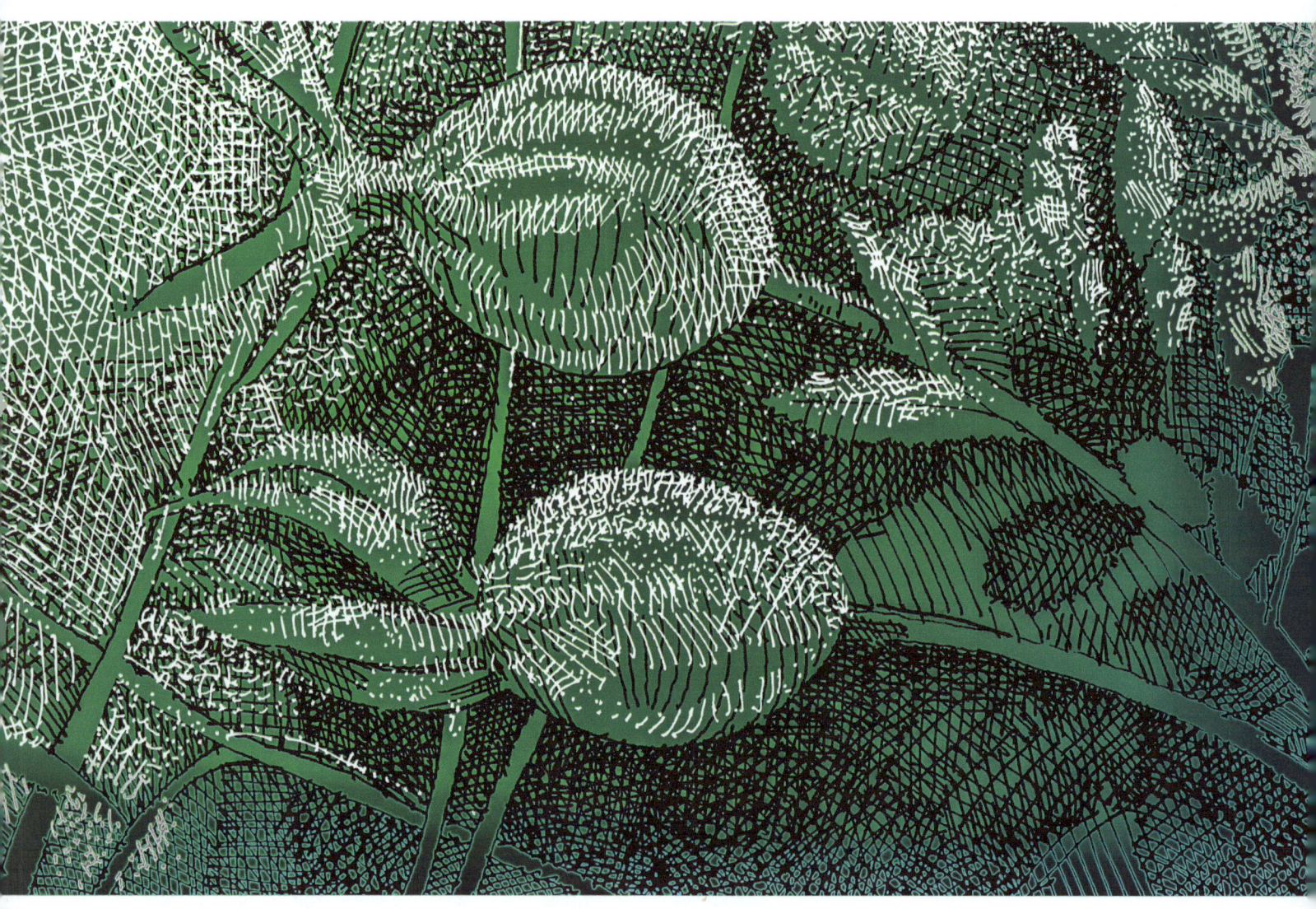

tender rose buds for deer to browse

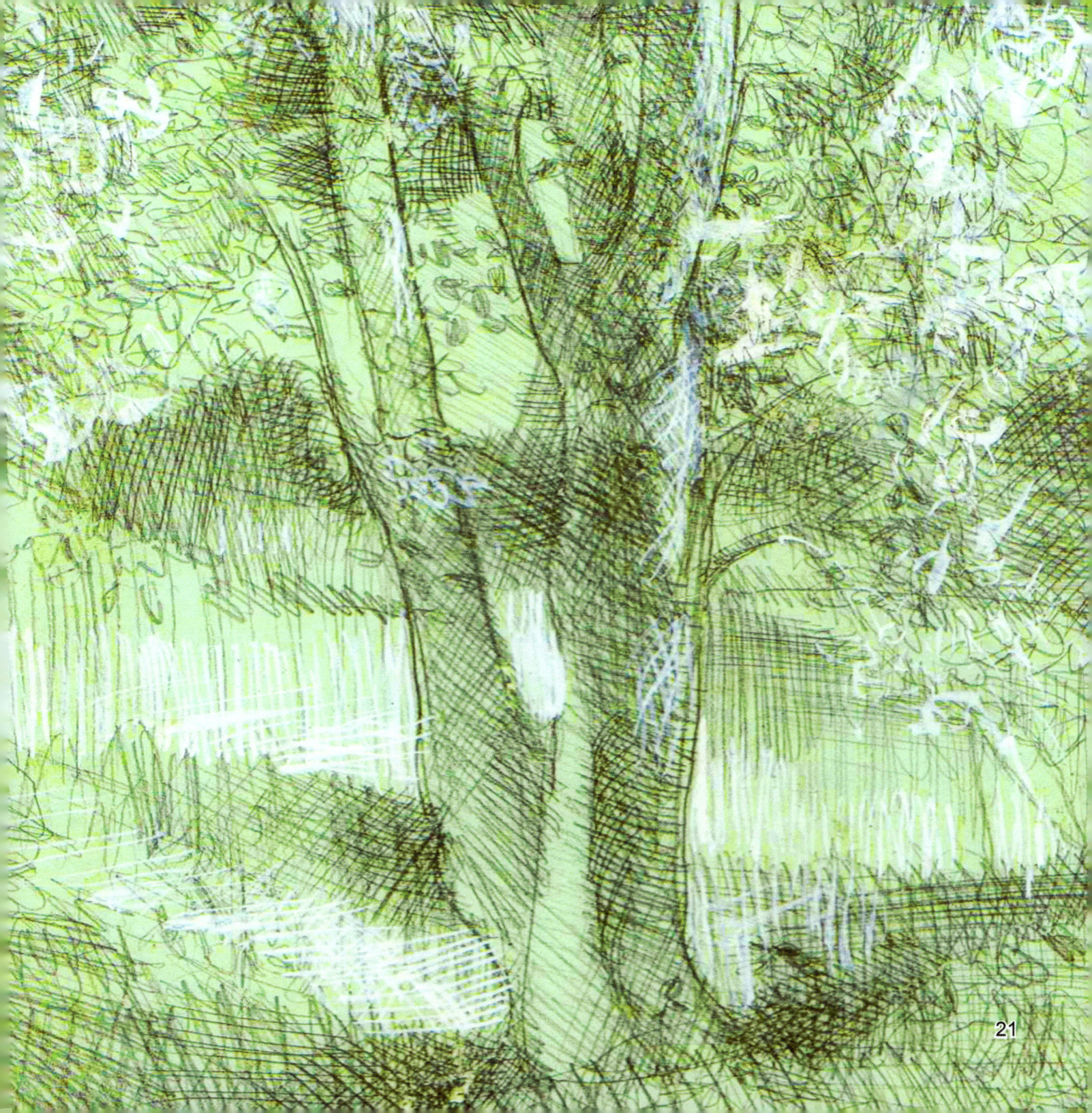

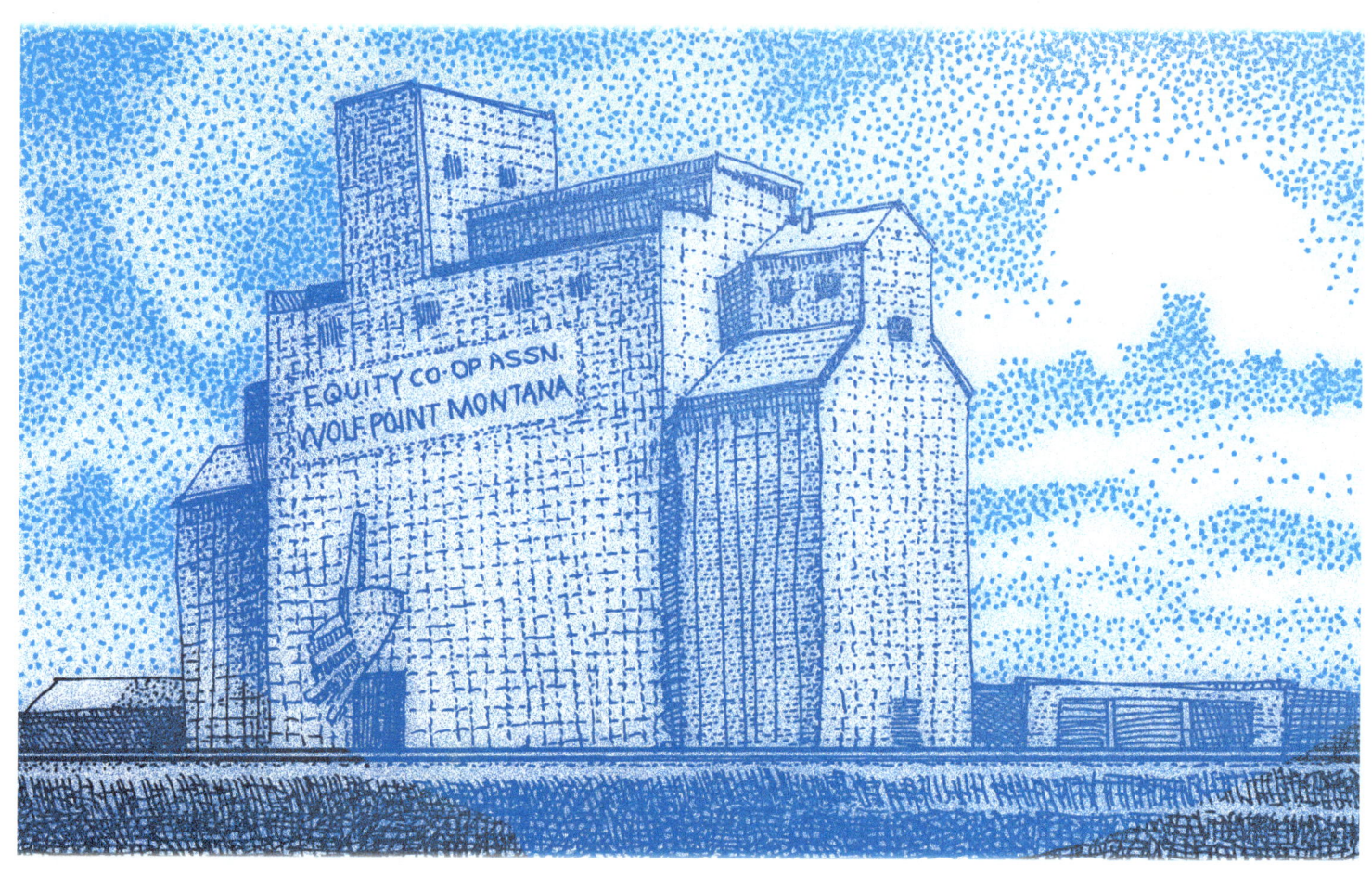

Glean.
Store.
Store and store grain.
Rails over grass send seeds to feed
    the center points of man.

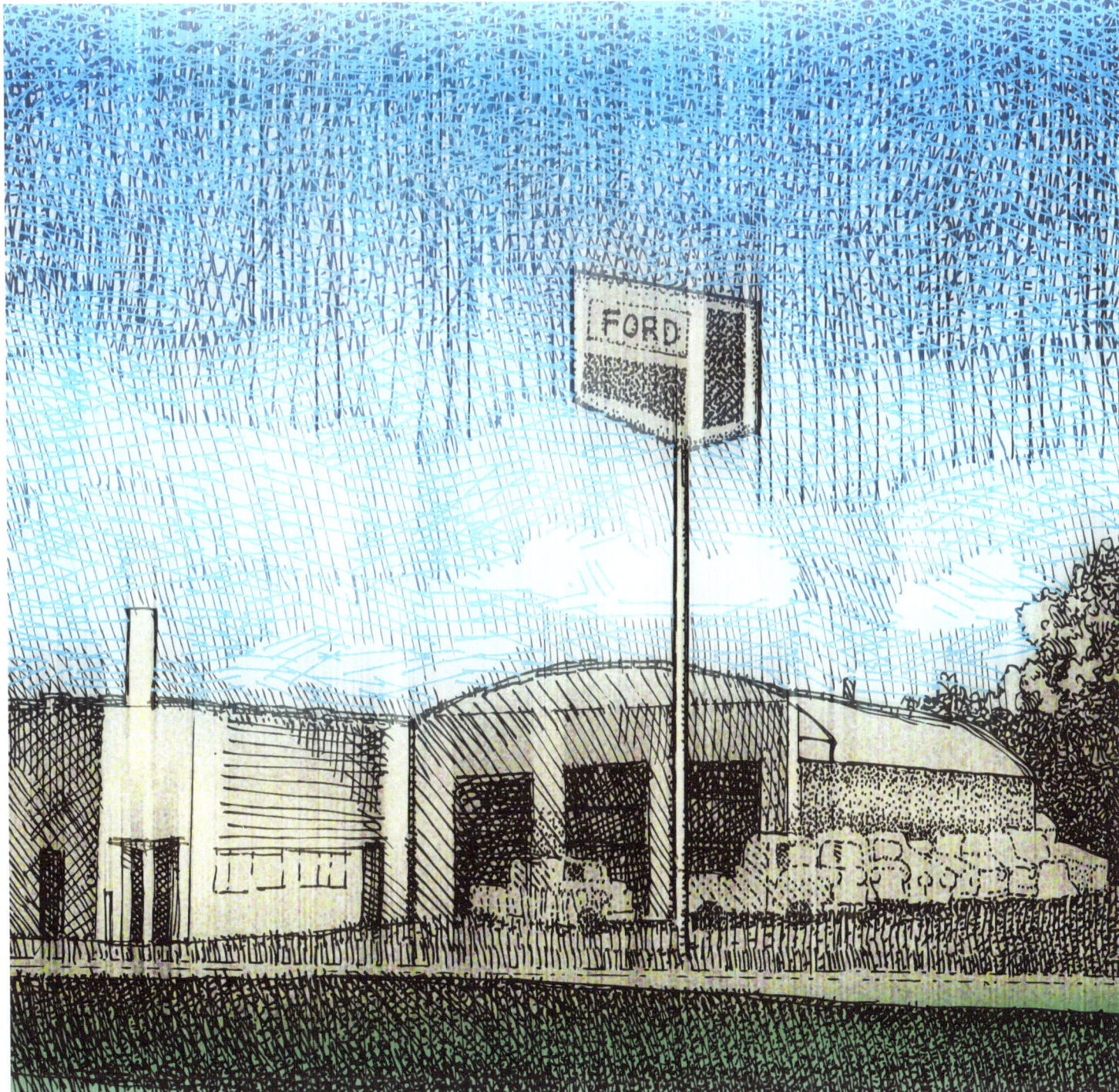

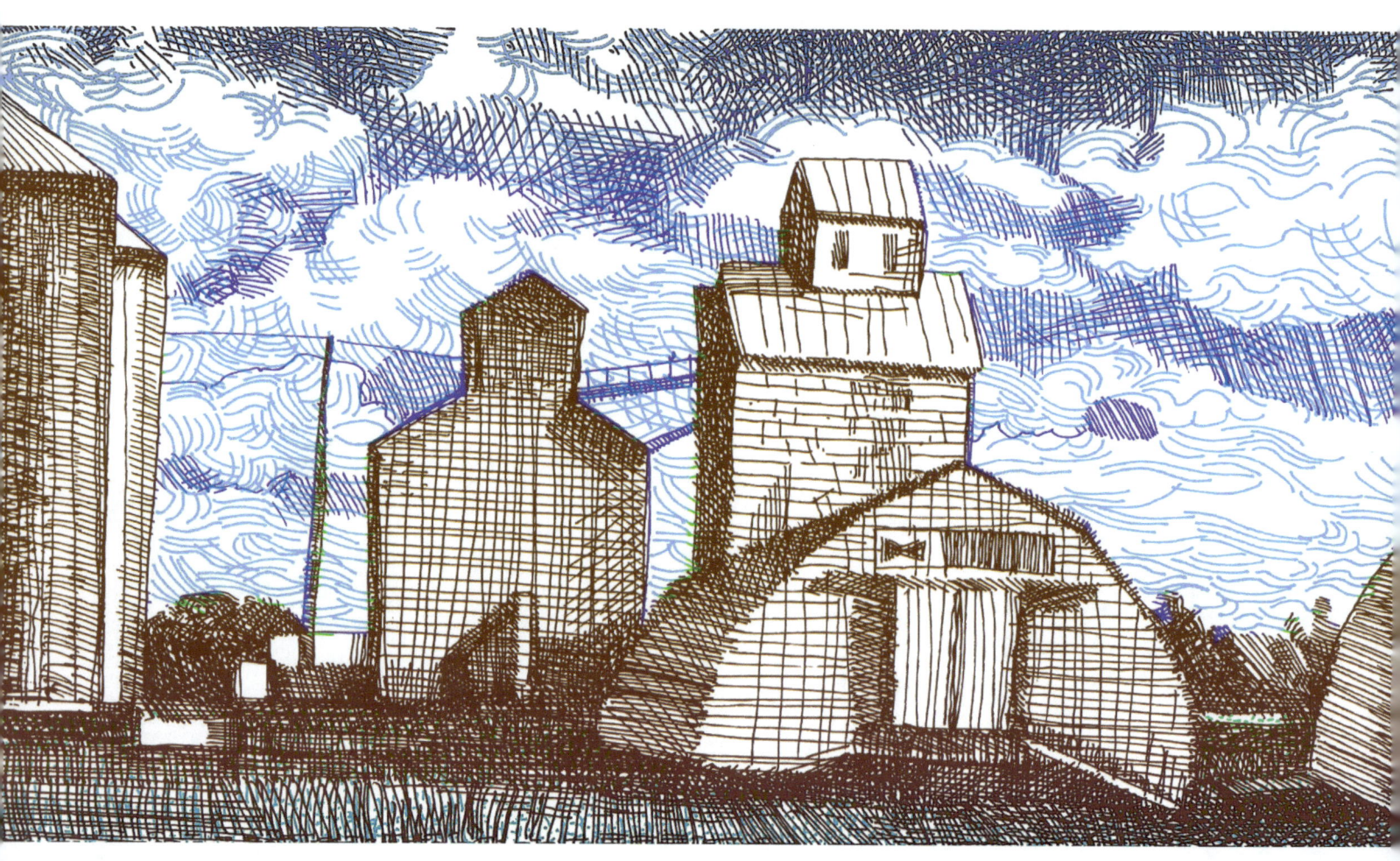

Store for the winter, for the cattle, for our horses.

24

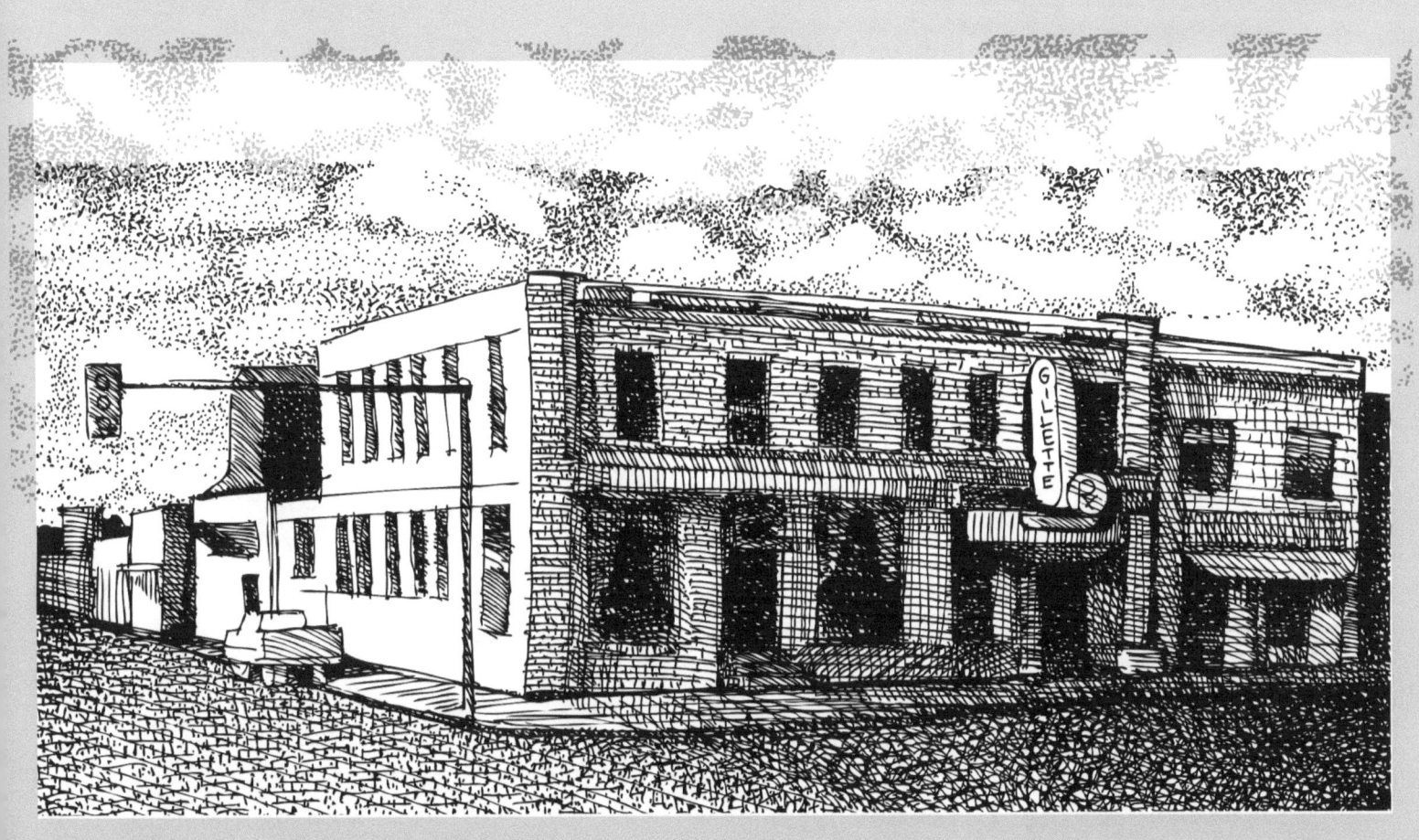

Hardware, groceries, drugs, dry goods, cafes, bars, car dealers, a theater, medical care, churches and schools

New York City on the Hudson
Wolf Point on the Missouri

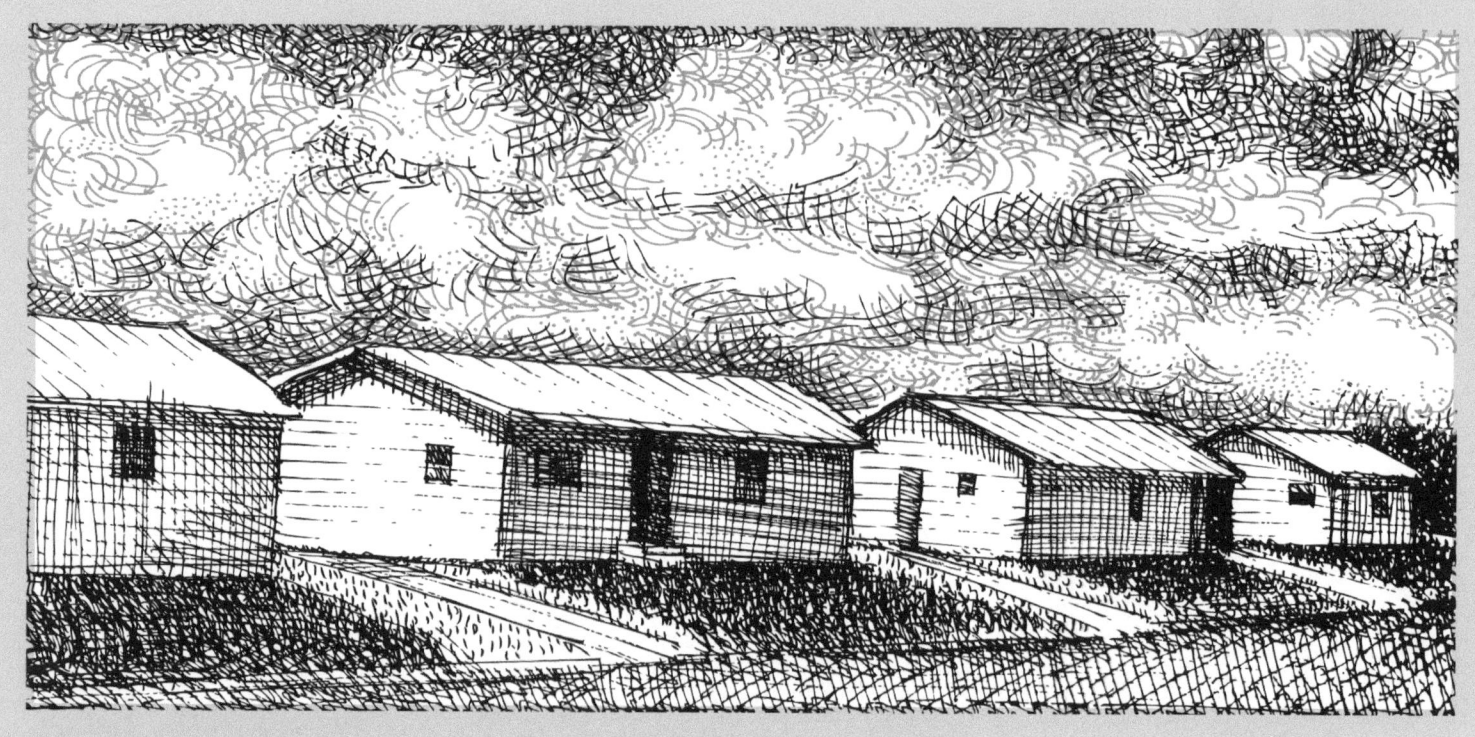

Simply live together in the grass.
Listen to its chant.
Measure silence.
　Then hear the legs of the
　beetle tickle the earth.

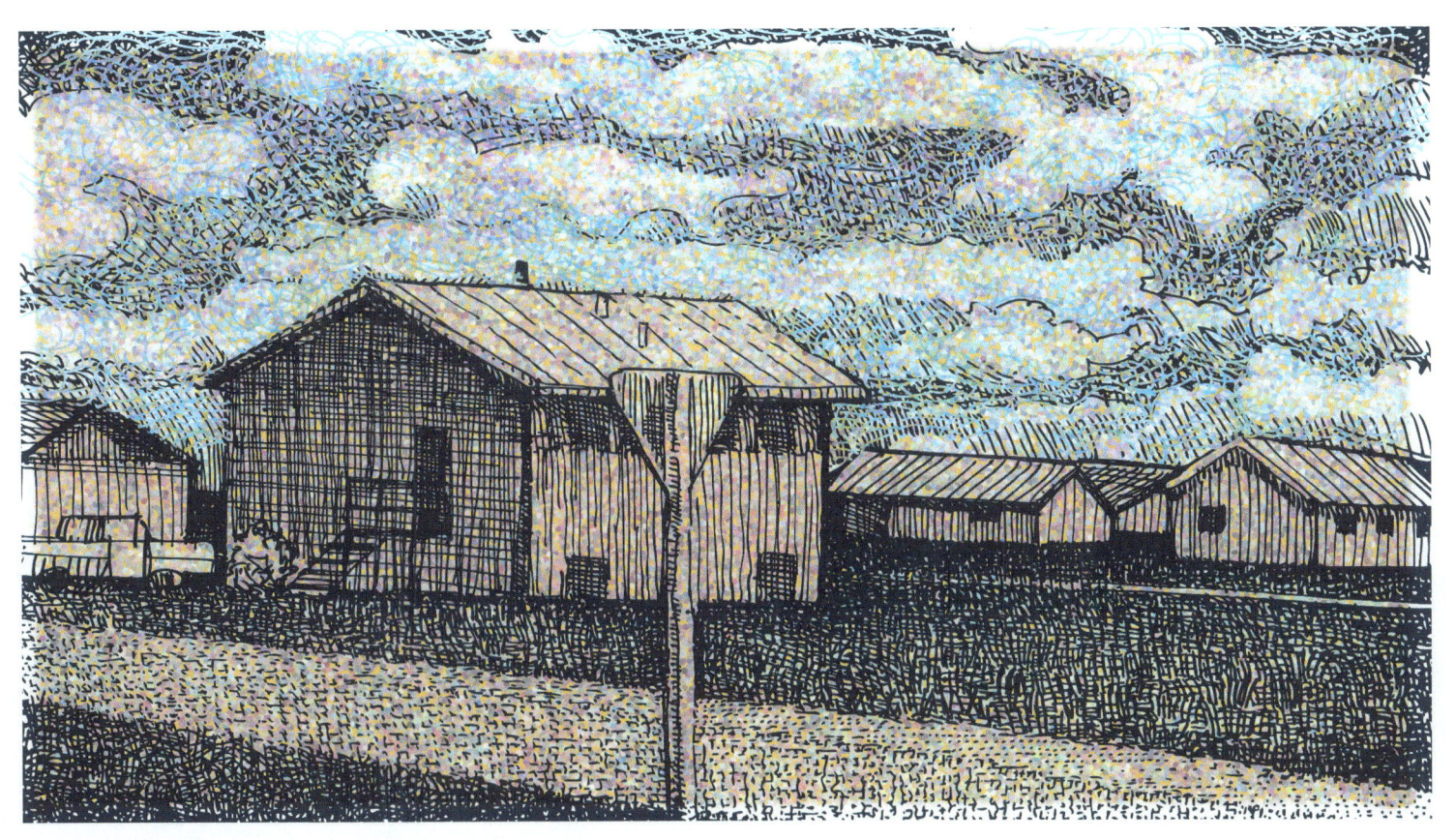

Assiniboine, Scandinavians, Sioux,
and English heritage

live side by side.

Ford, GM, and Ram
pickups create everyone equal.

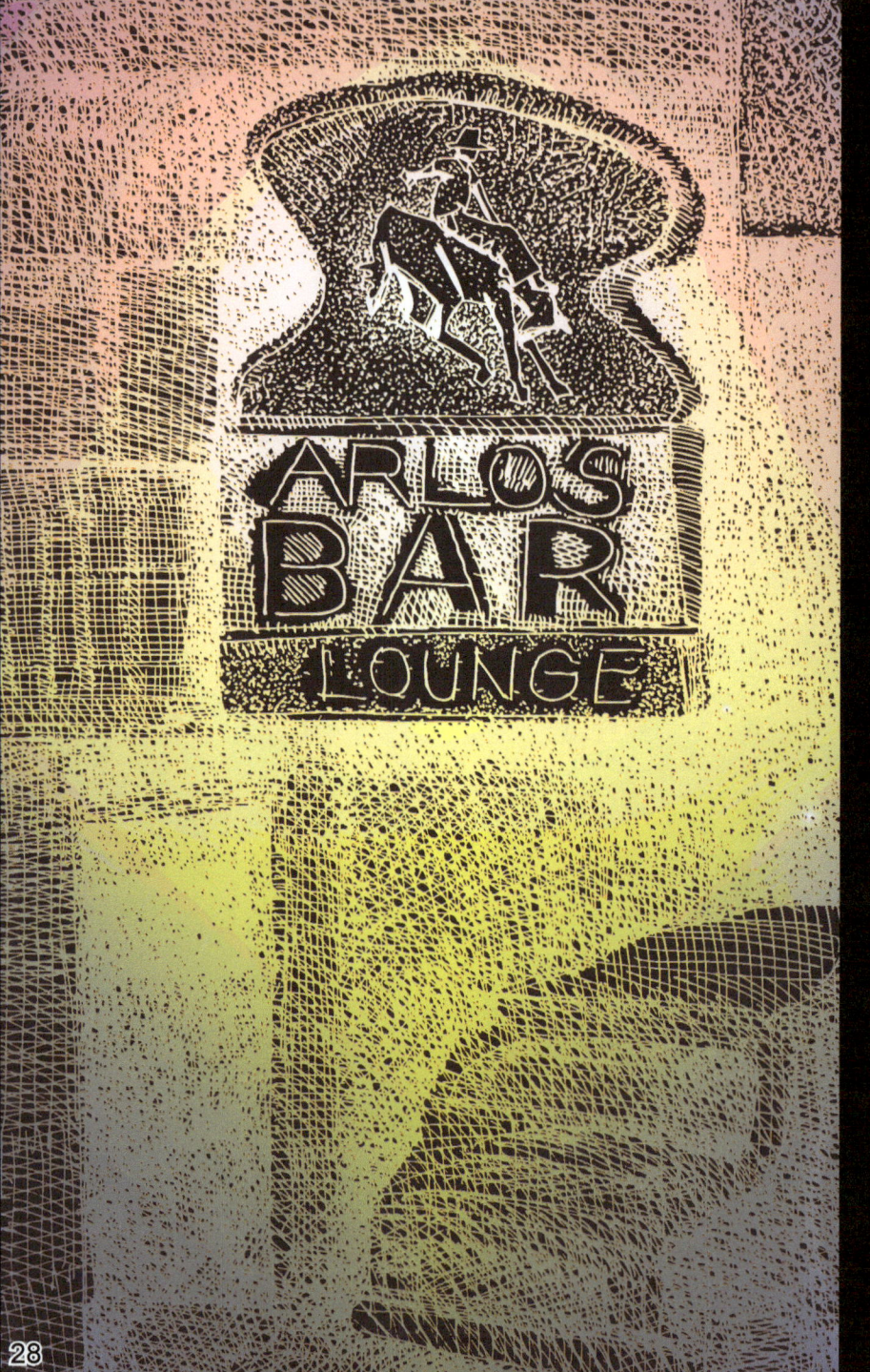

After the witching hour
   the night glows neon.
Cloister.
Hide from the moon,
   stars,
   night clouds,
   endless land.

A small, warm world
   lies close.
Space understood.
Bodies long to blur
   isolation.
Touch.

In the morning
   space looms.

Sorrows grow
as crops.
We remember
both, empty
and full.

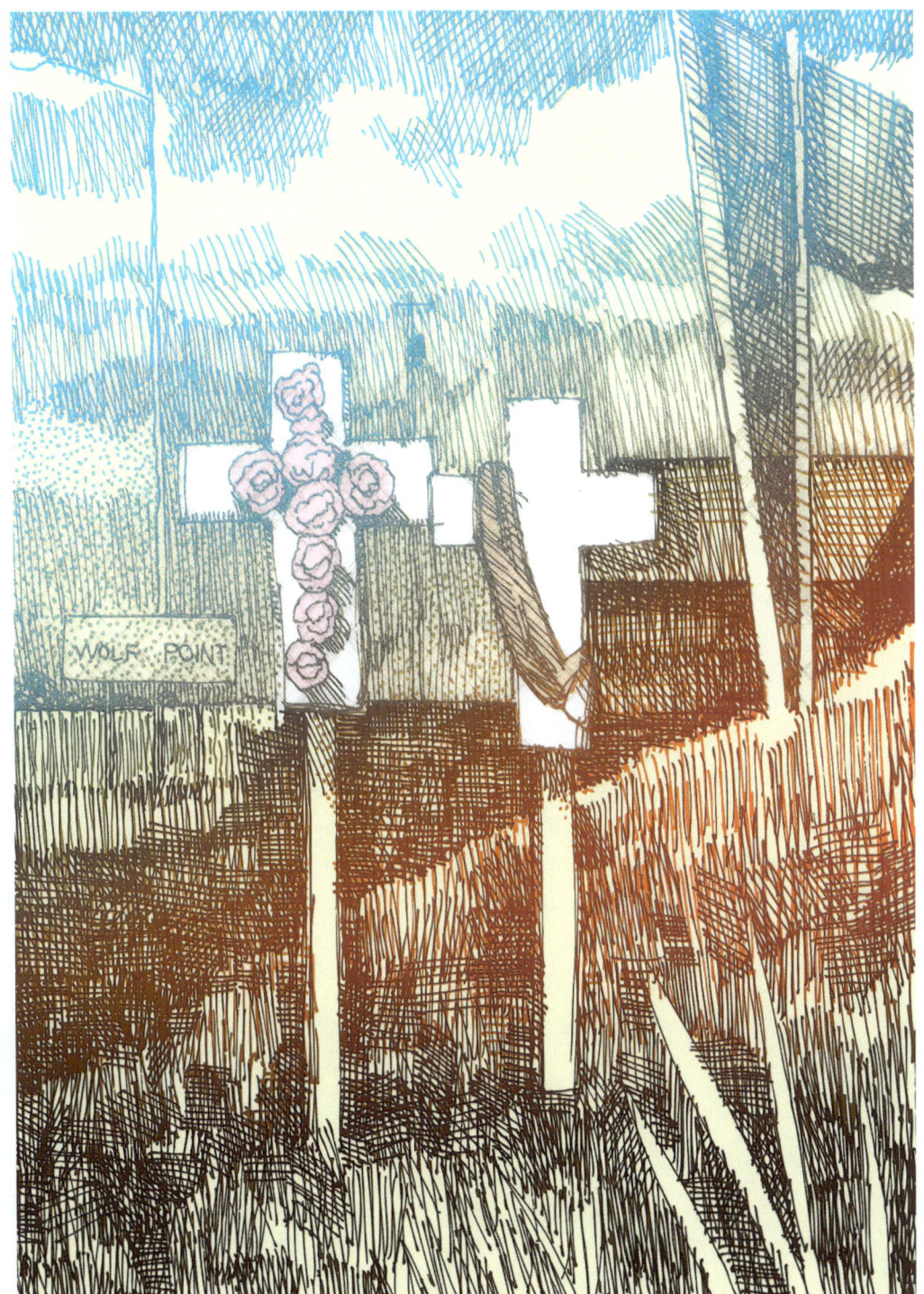

29

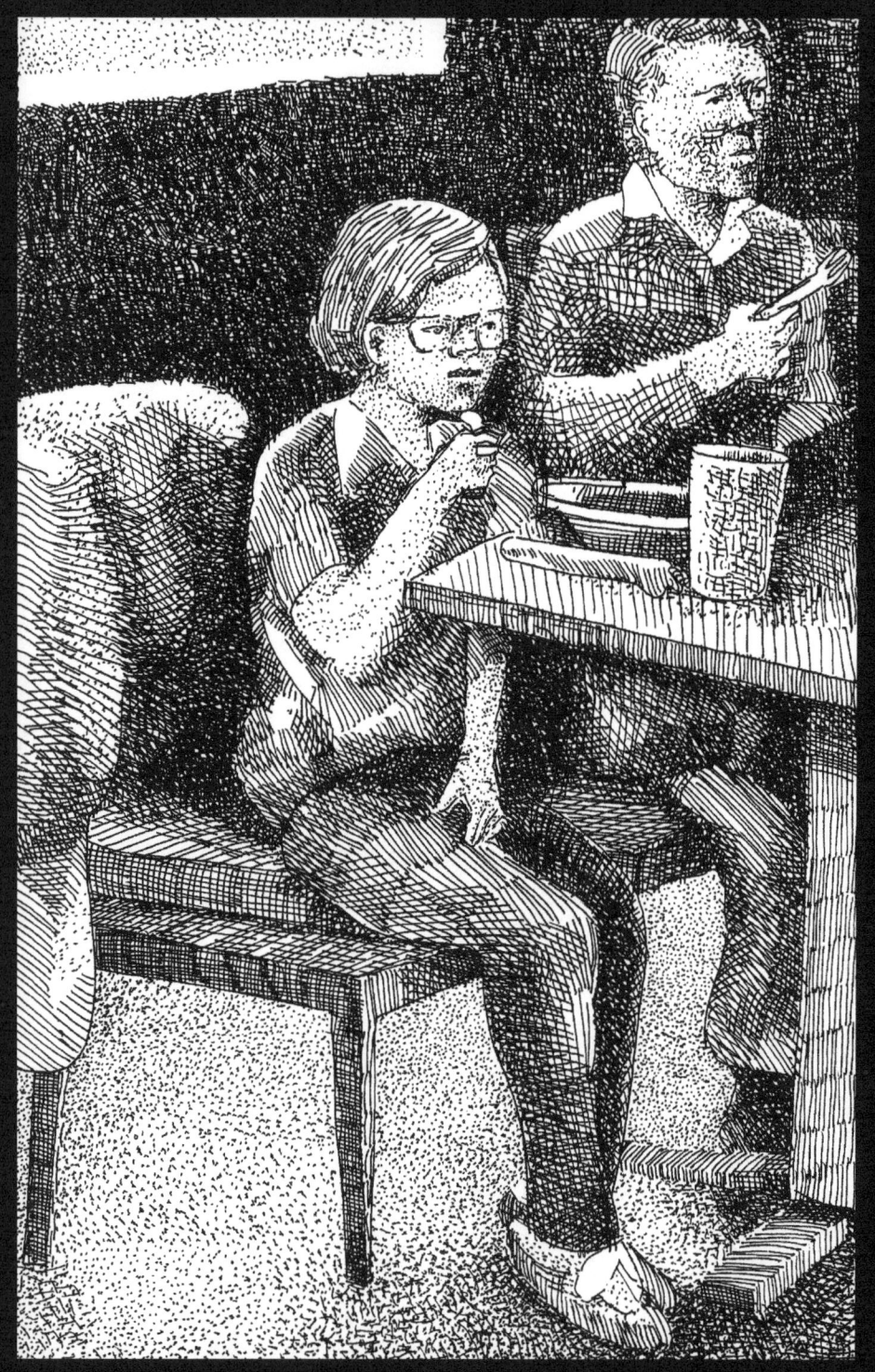

Creature people
of the plains
create family.

In small prides
they gather,
water, and
feed:
unity of
moment.

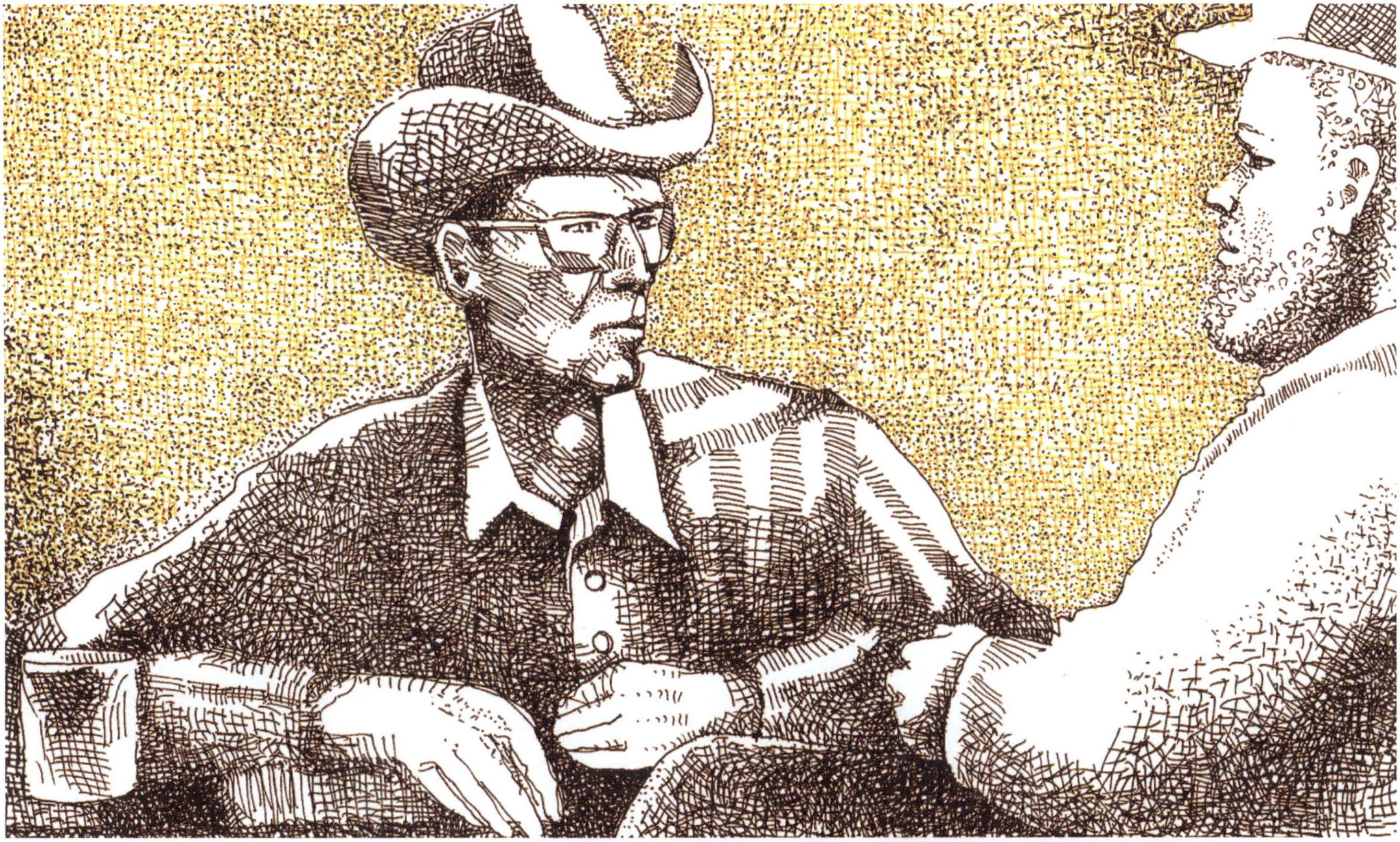

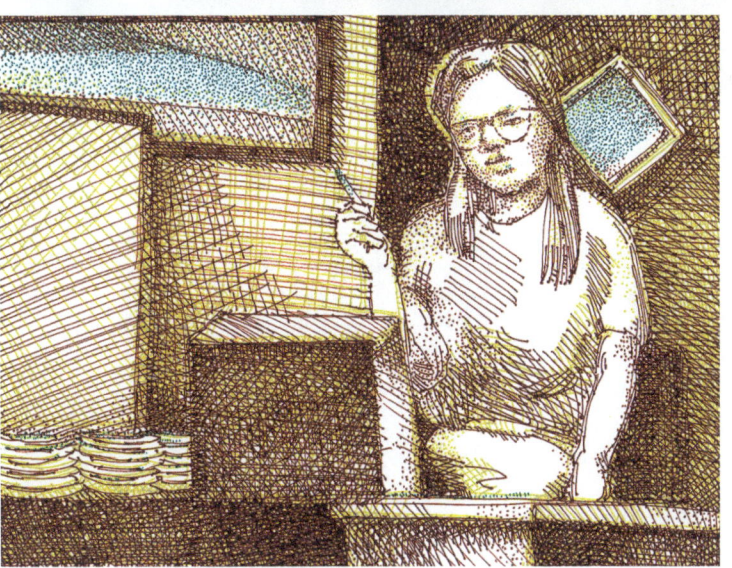

At the Stockman's Cafe leathered men chew coffee. Speak: Weather, Tractor, Cattle Cube, Tax, Gas Price, and other languages as required.

Cecil breaks for a smoke.

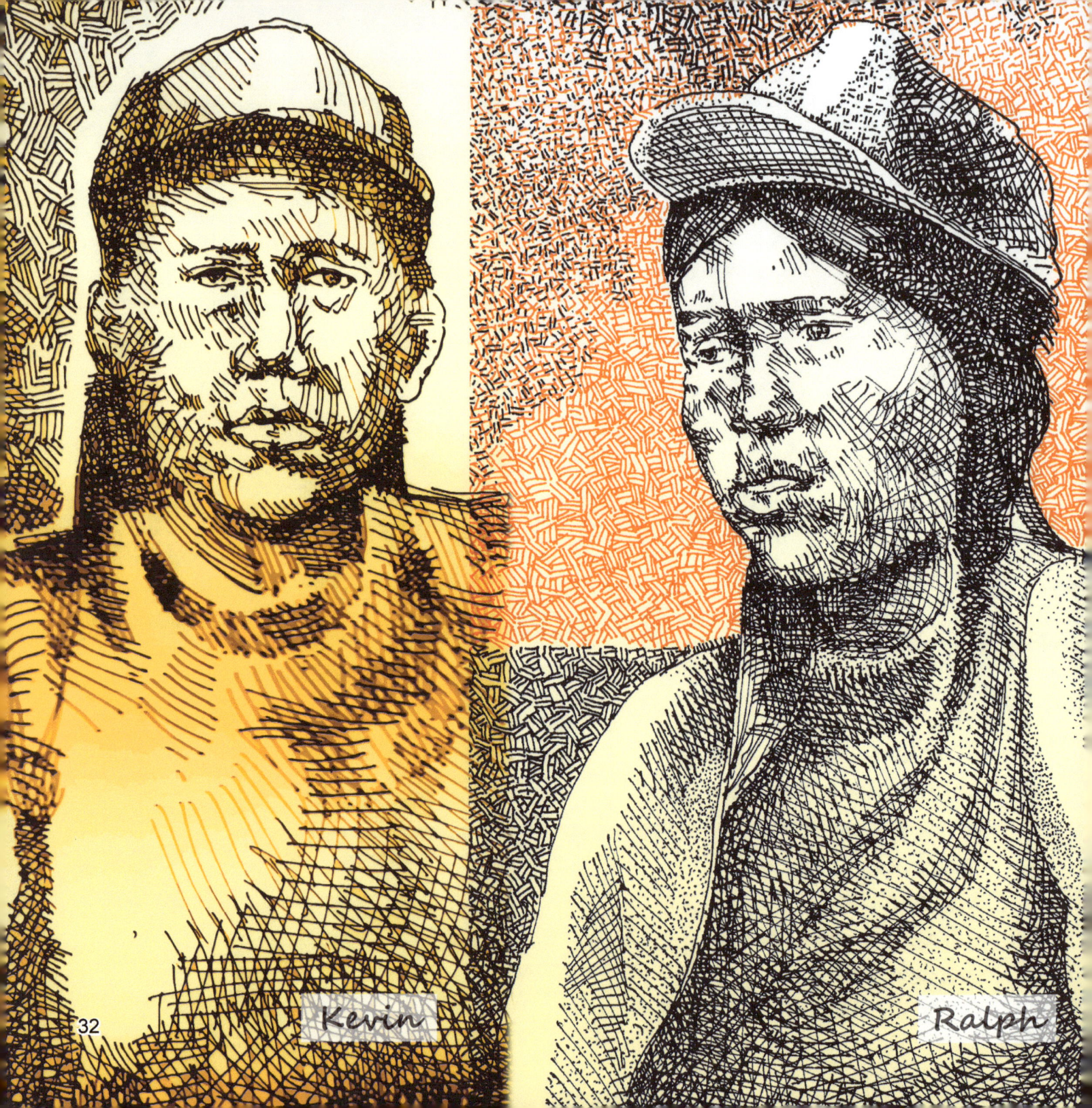

32 Kevin Ralph

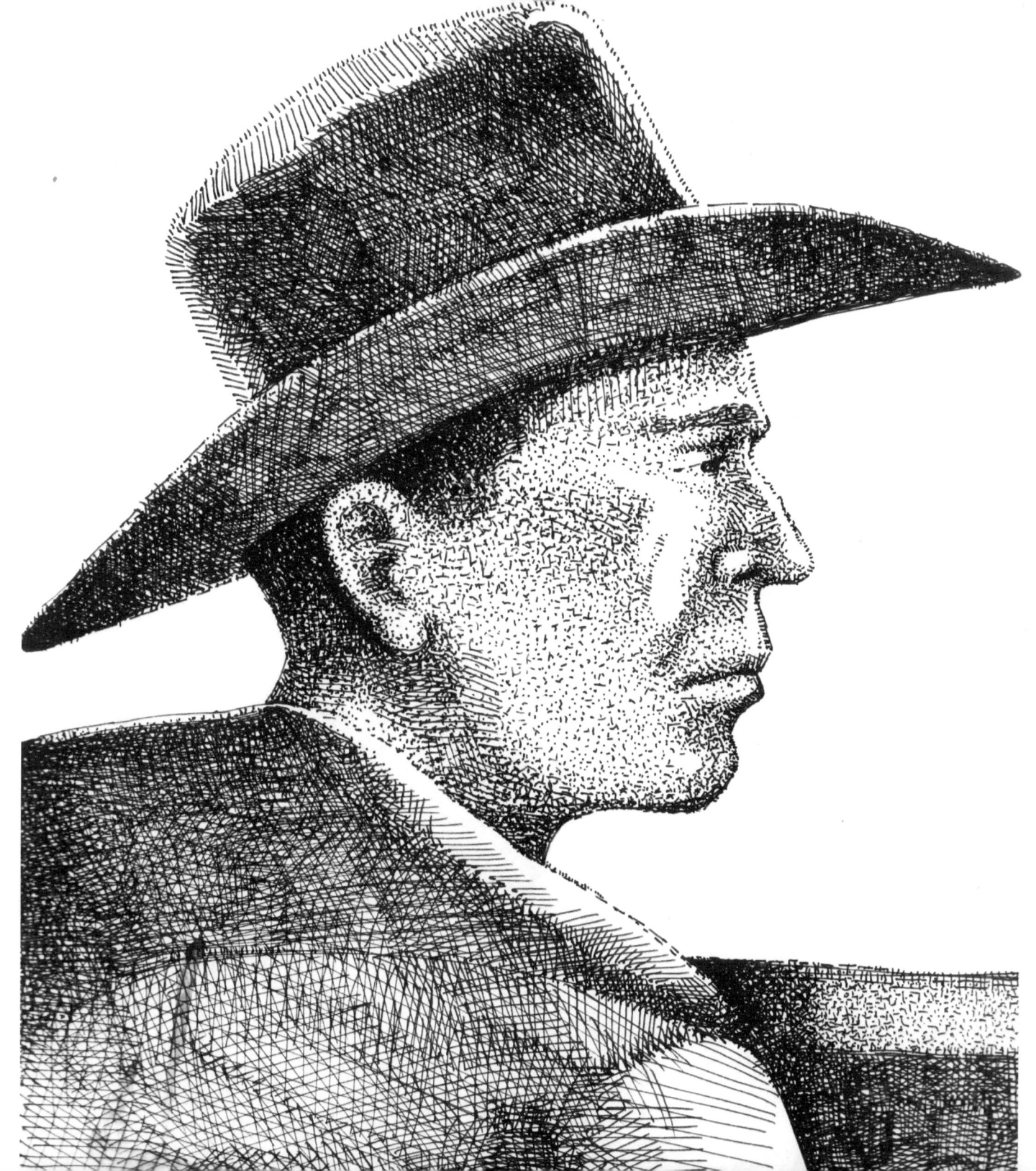

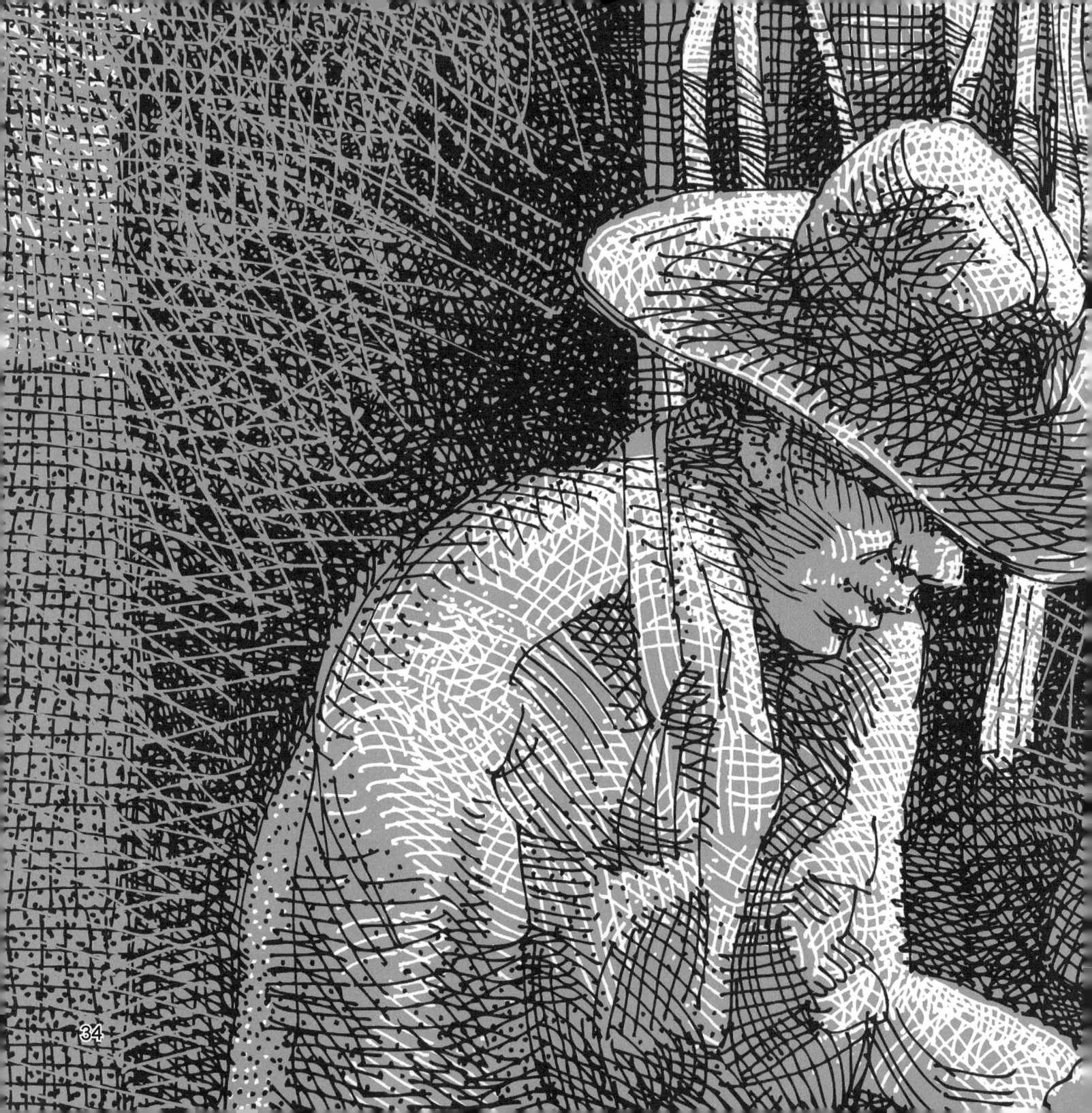

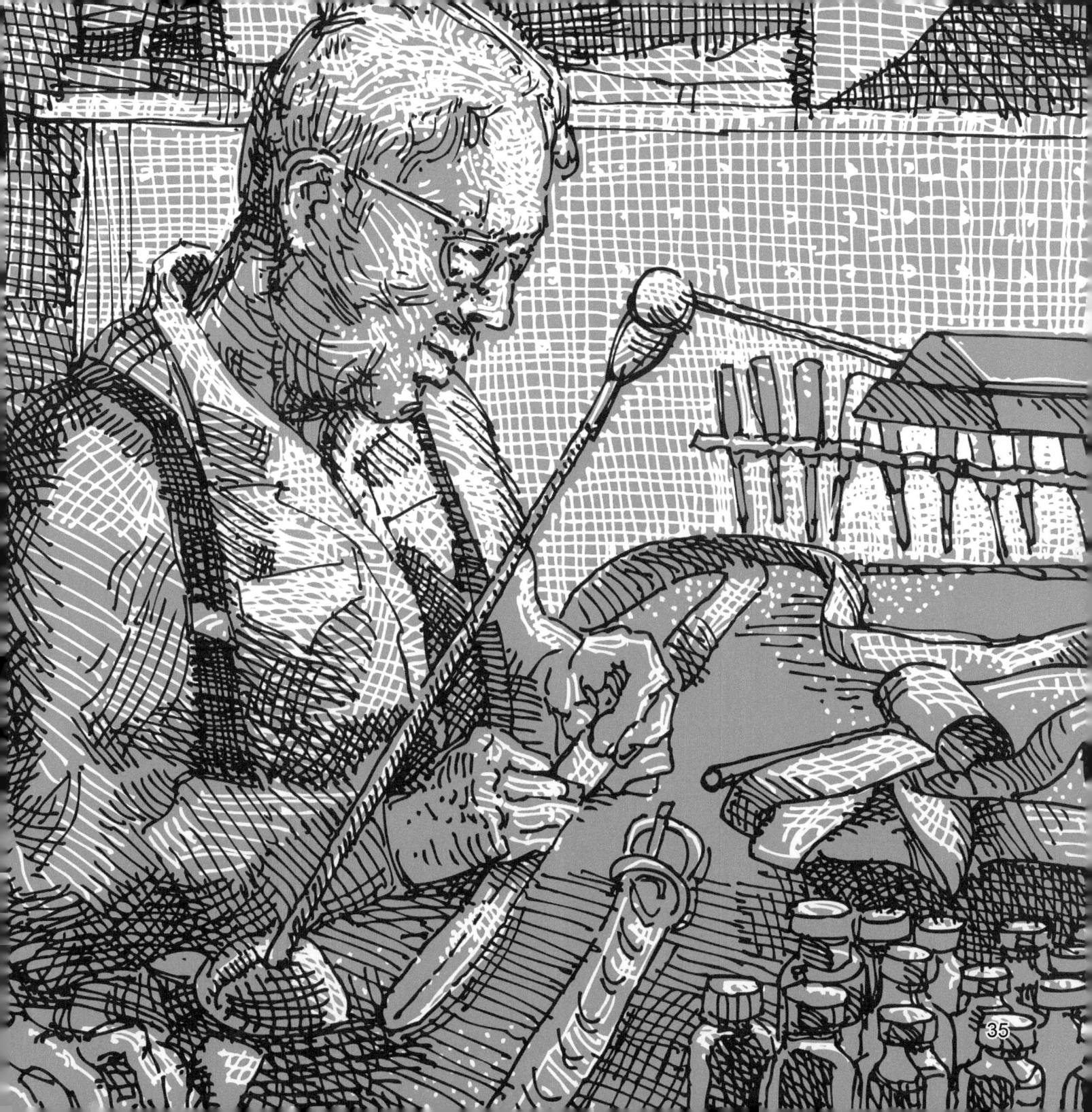

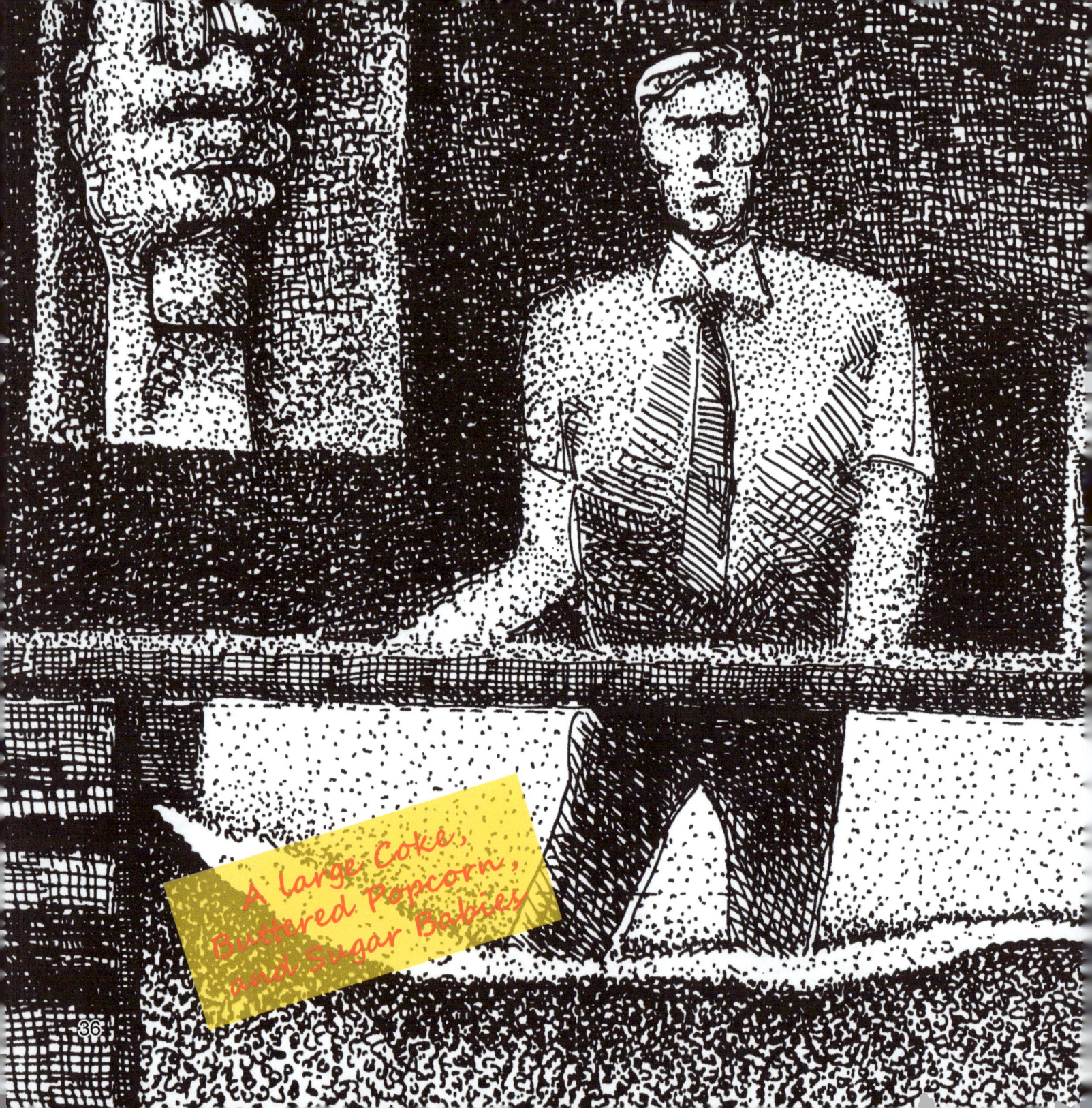

A large Coke, Buttered Popcorn, and Sugar Babies

36

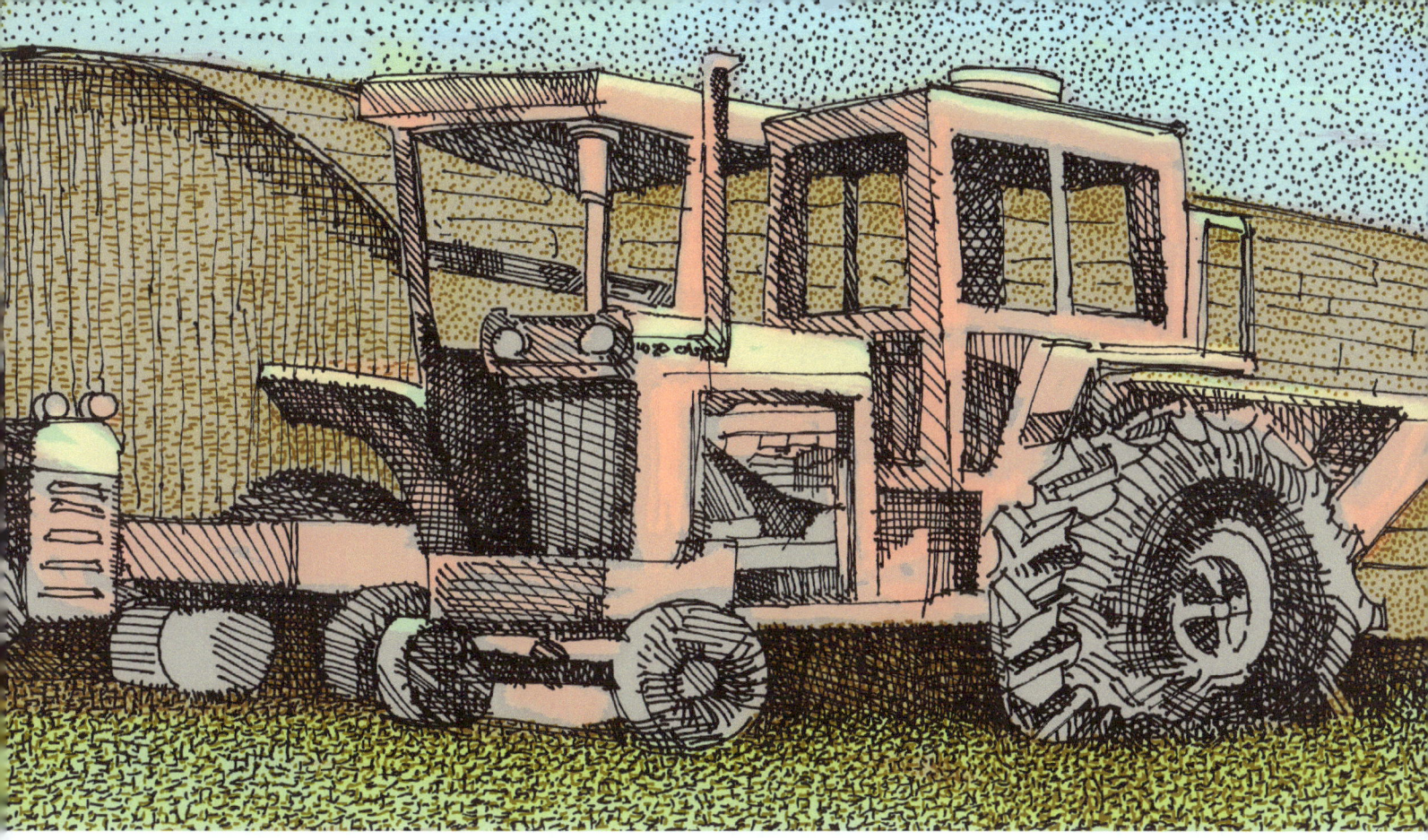

Machines range the praire,
as past great oxen, draft horses, and mules.
In herds they harvest.
We bake.

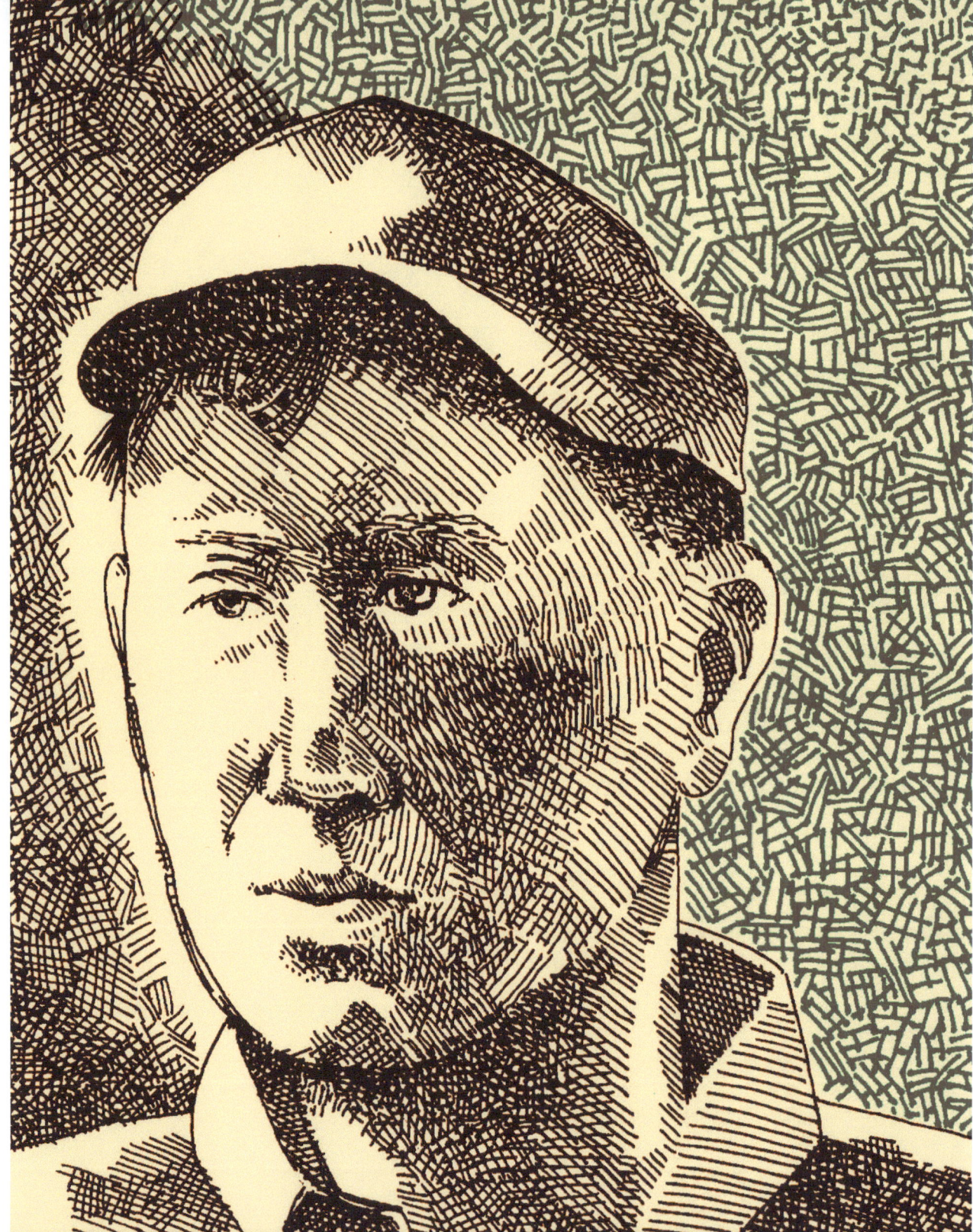

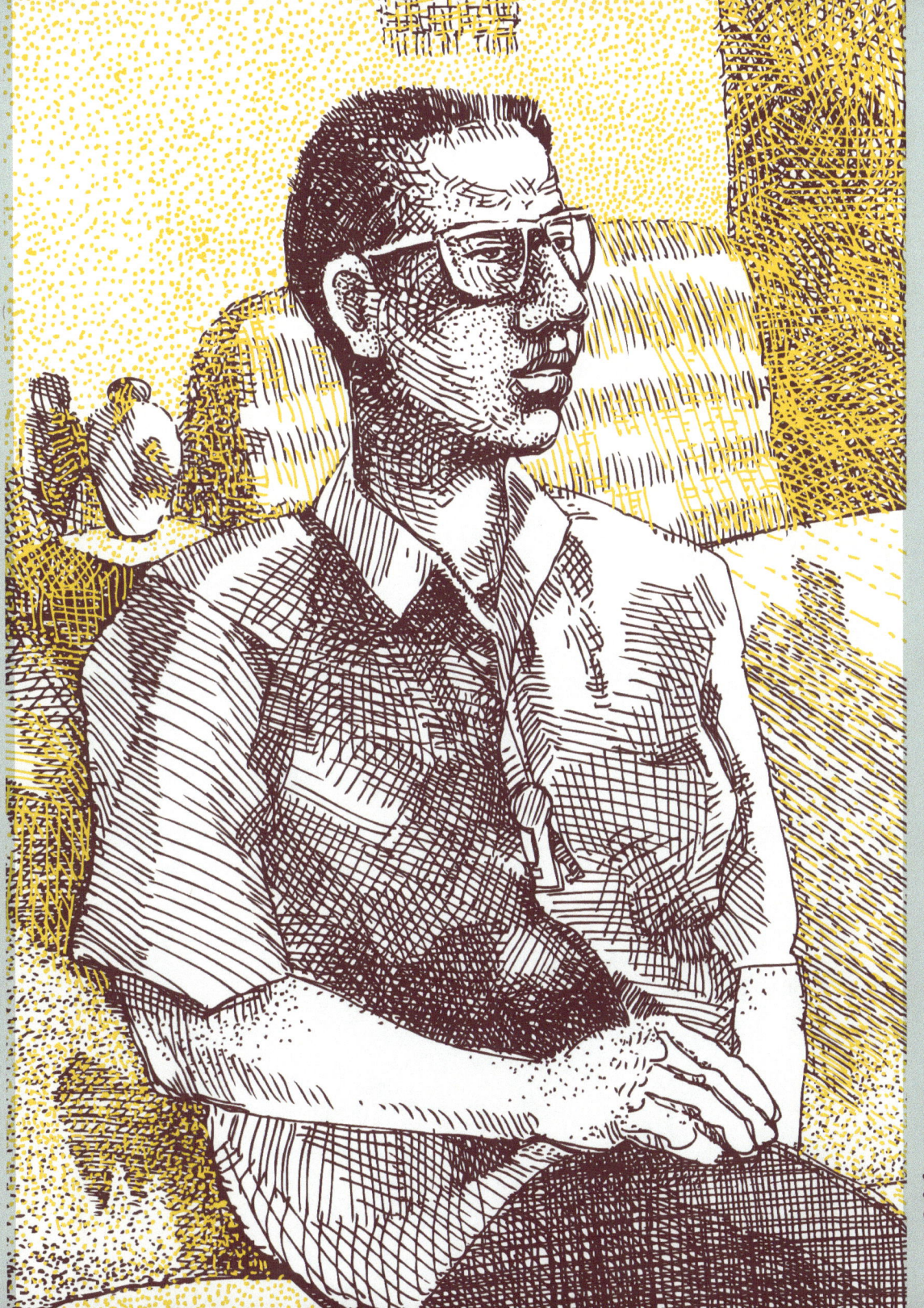

Clinton

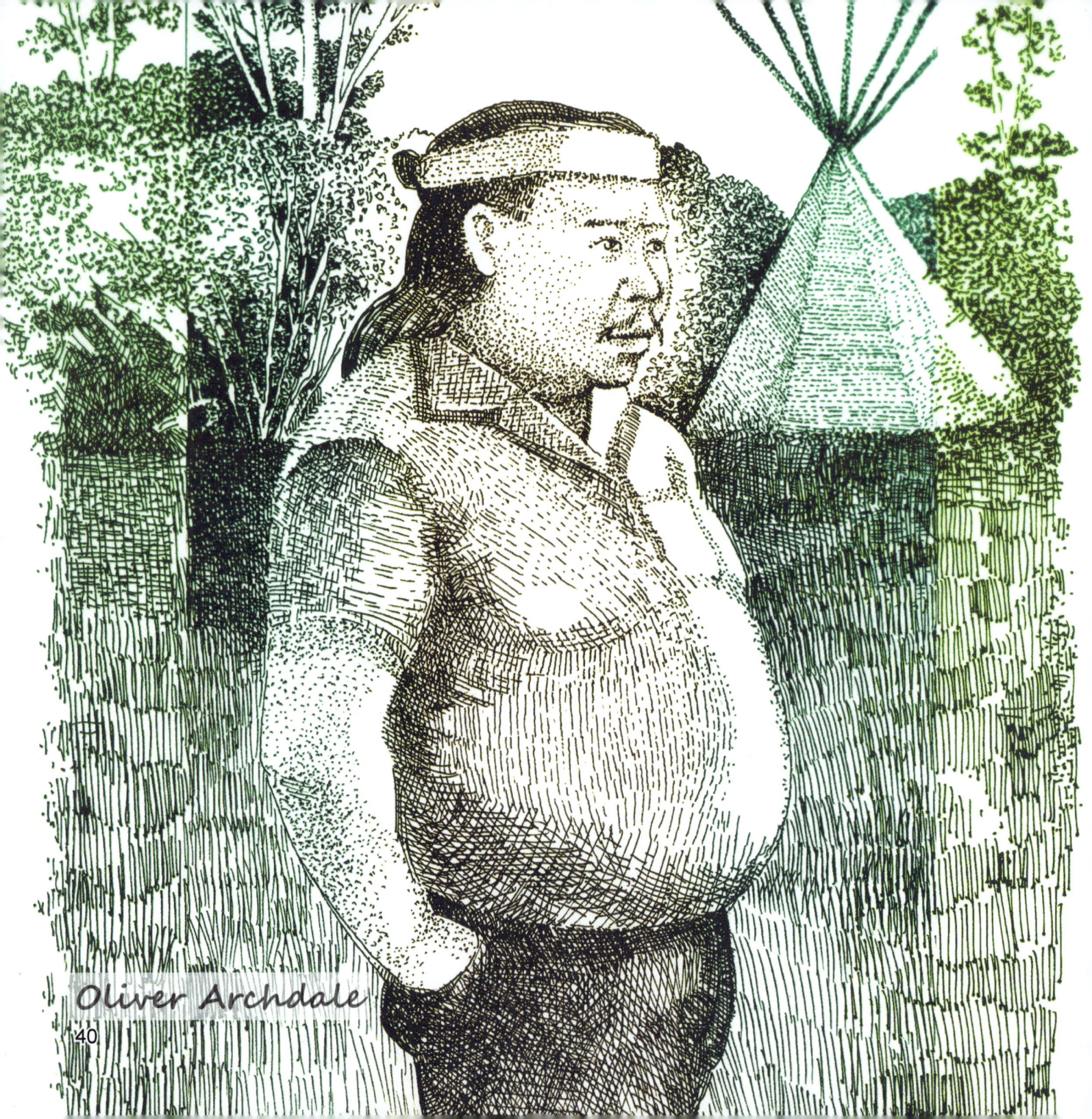

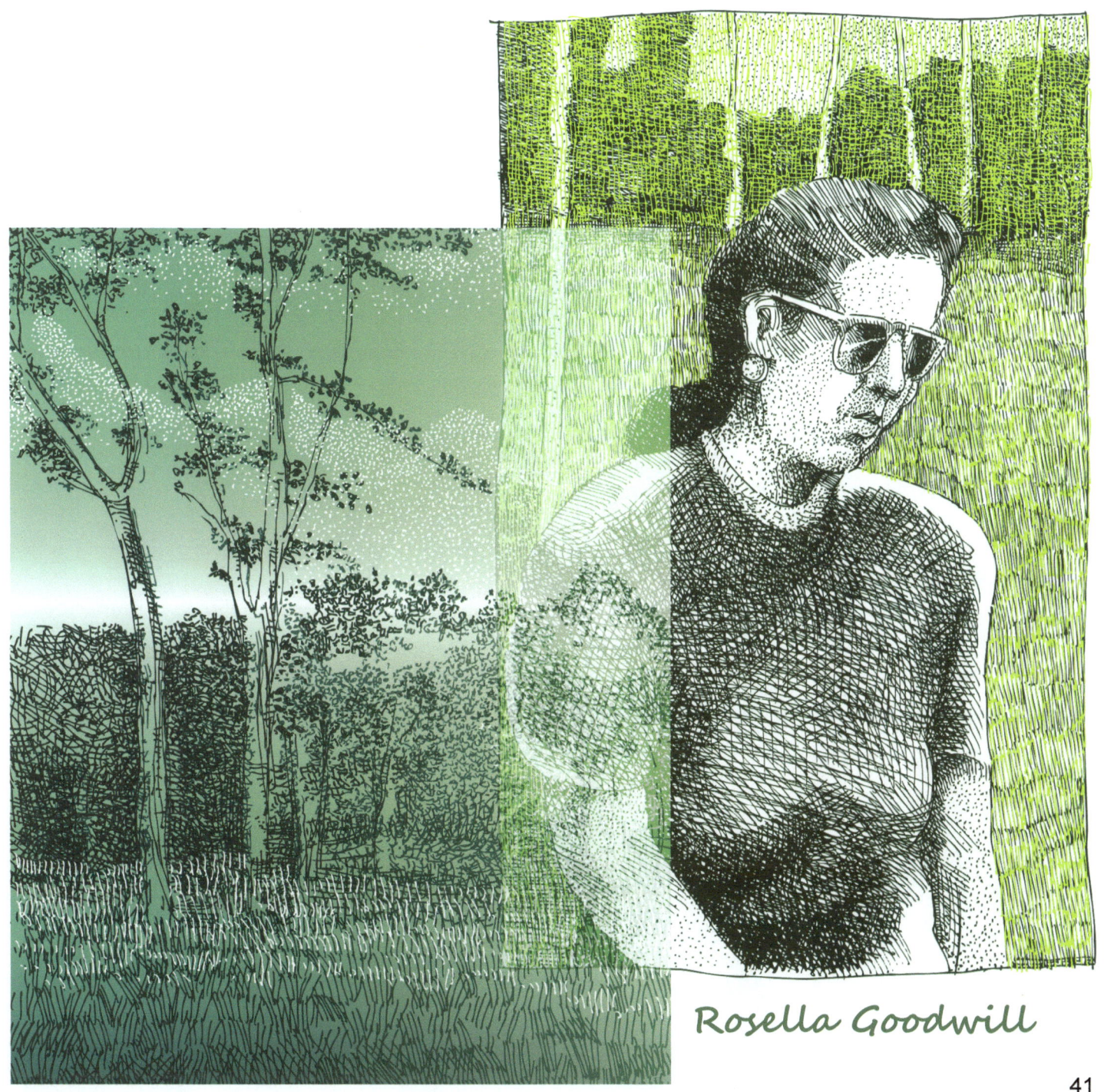

Rosella Goodwill

41

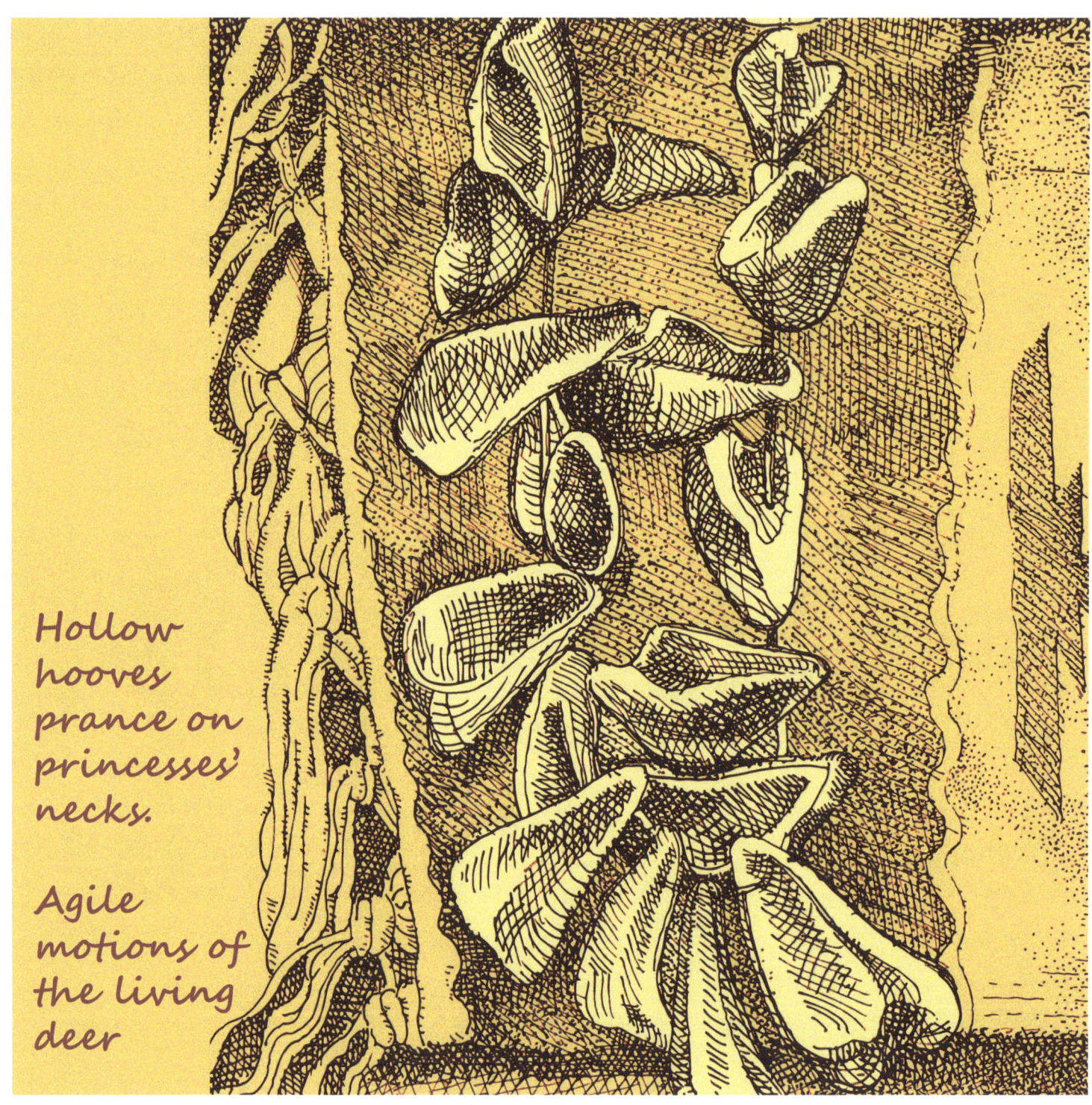

Hollow
hooves
prance on
princesses'
necks.

Agile
motions of
the living
deer

Rosella creates heritage for a young girl.

What have I been? What am I now? Who will I be?

43

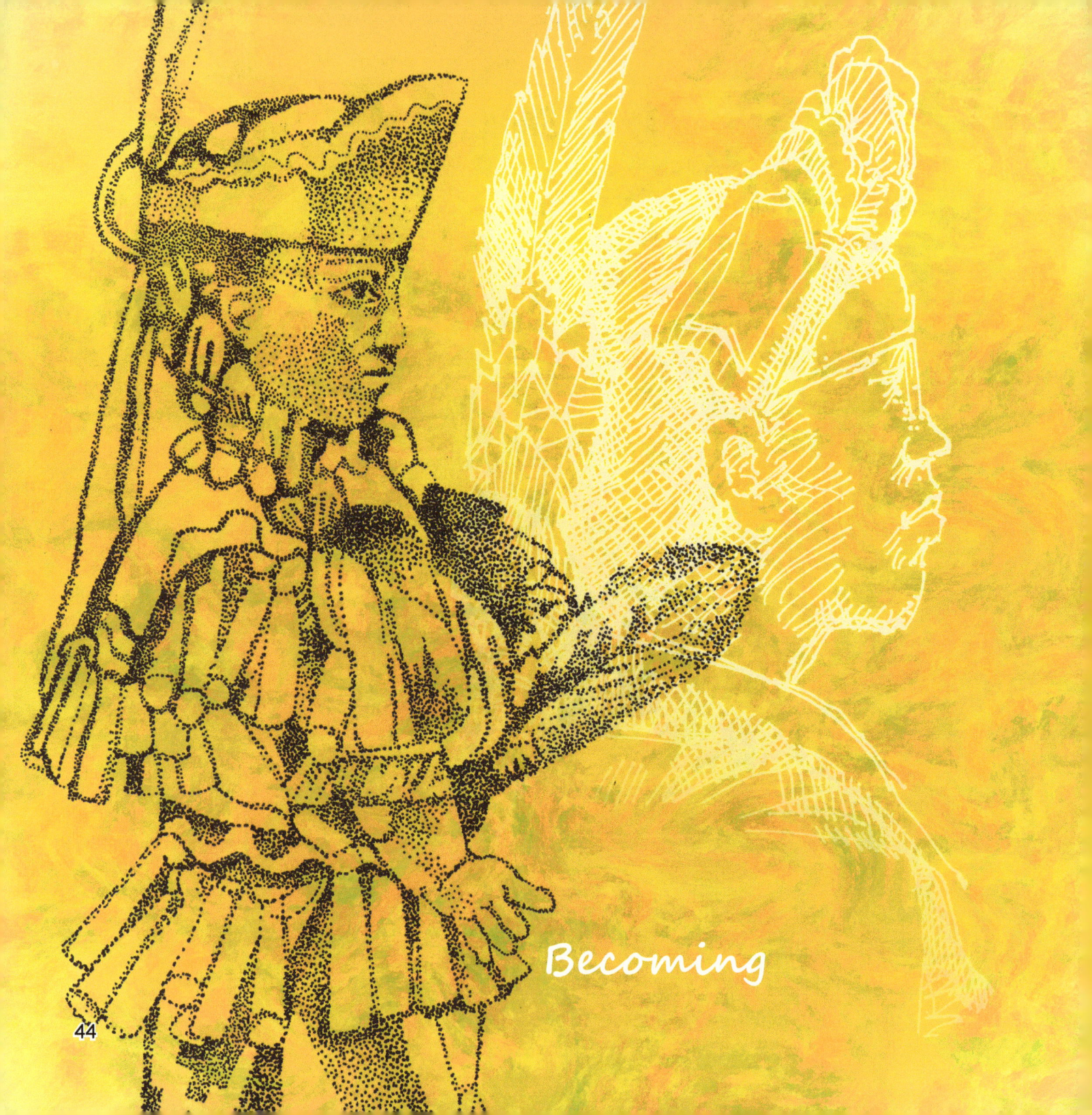

Becoming

44

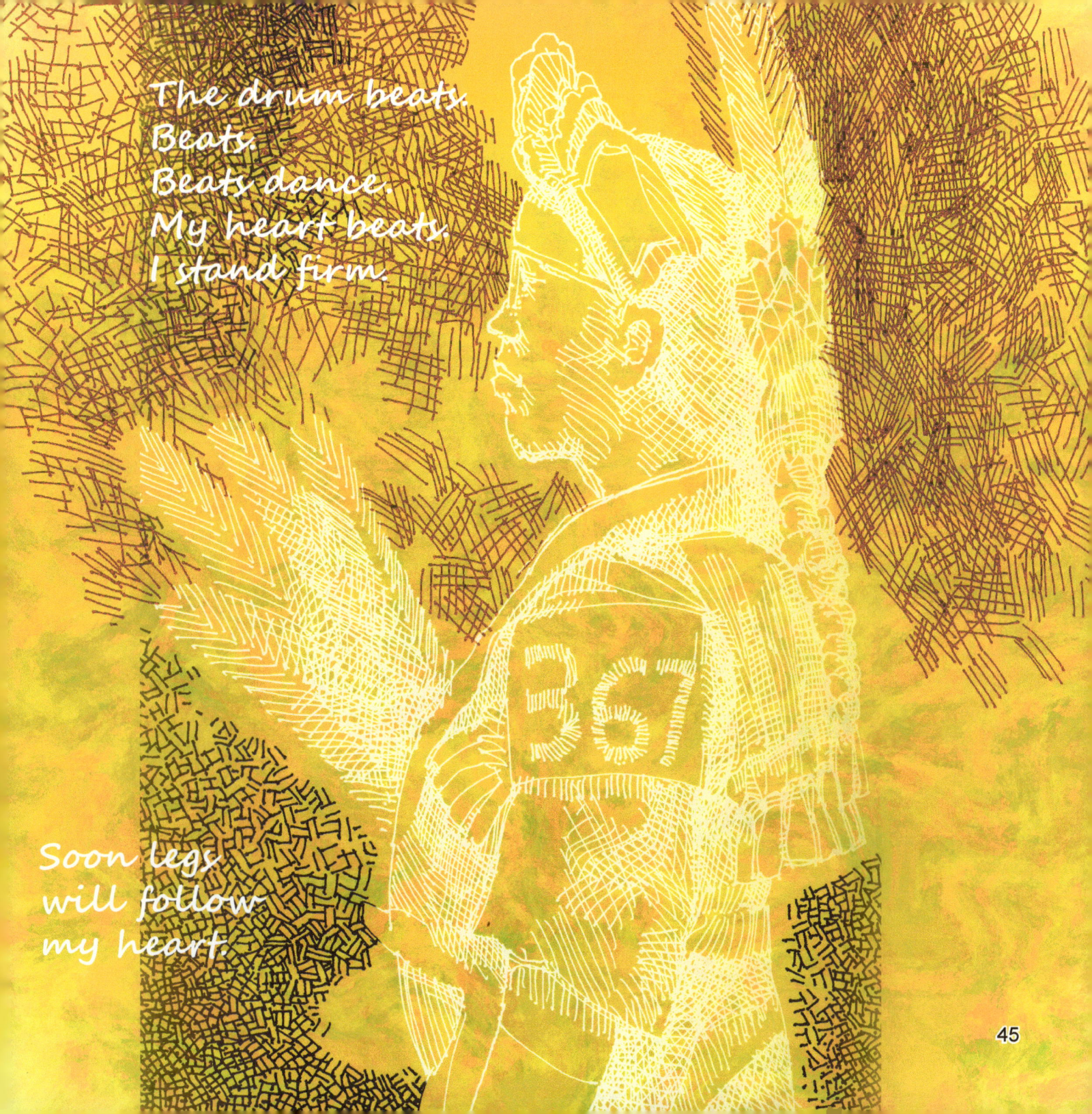

The drum beats.
Beats.
Beats dance.
My heart beats.
I stand firm.

Soon legs
will follow
my heart.

45

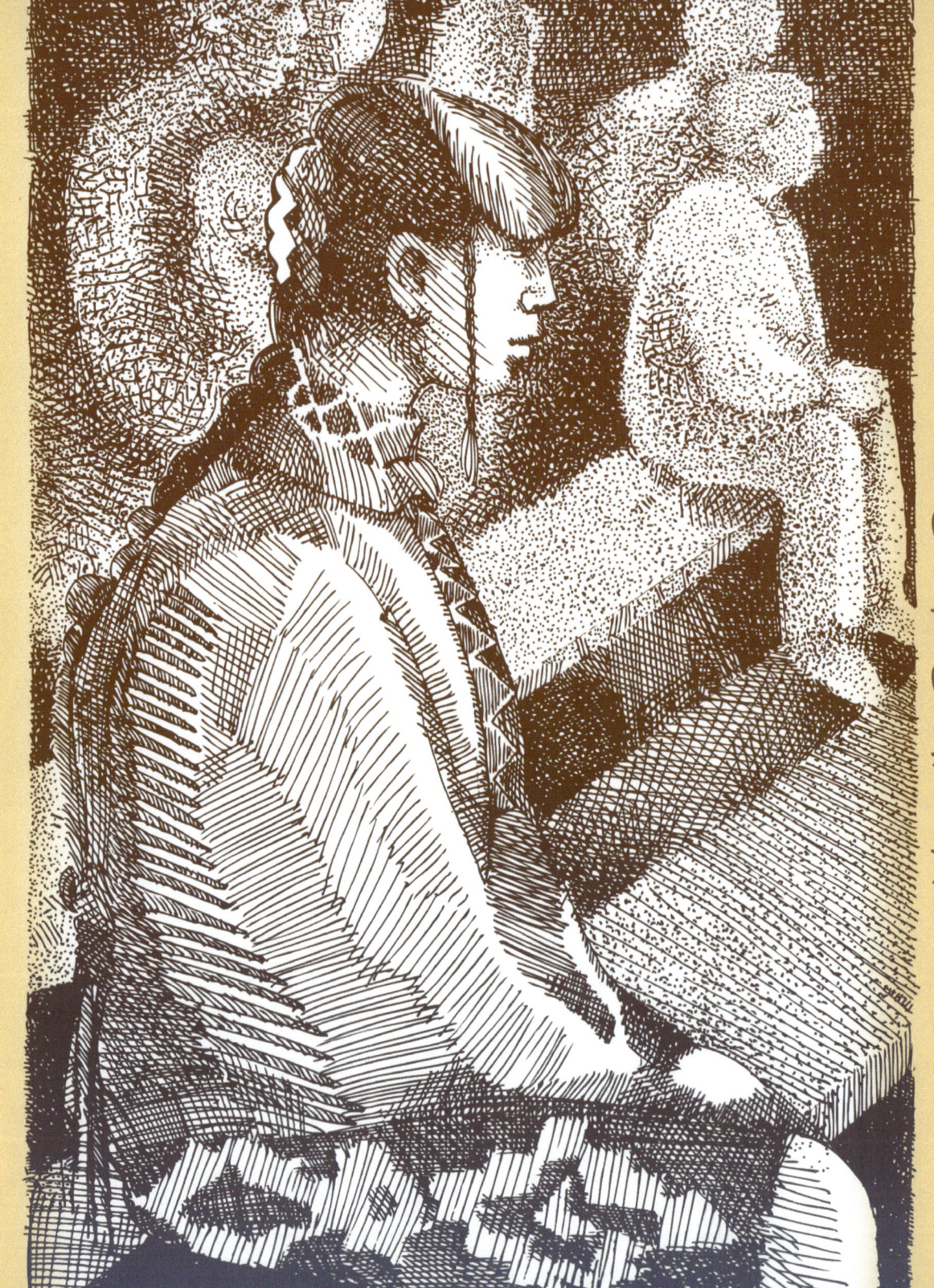

June watches the Poplar Powwow.

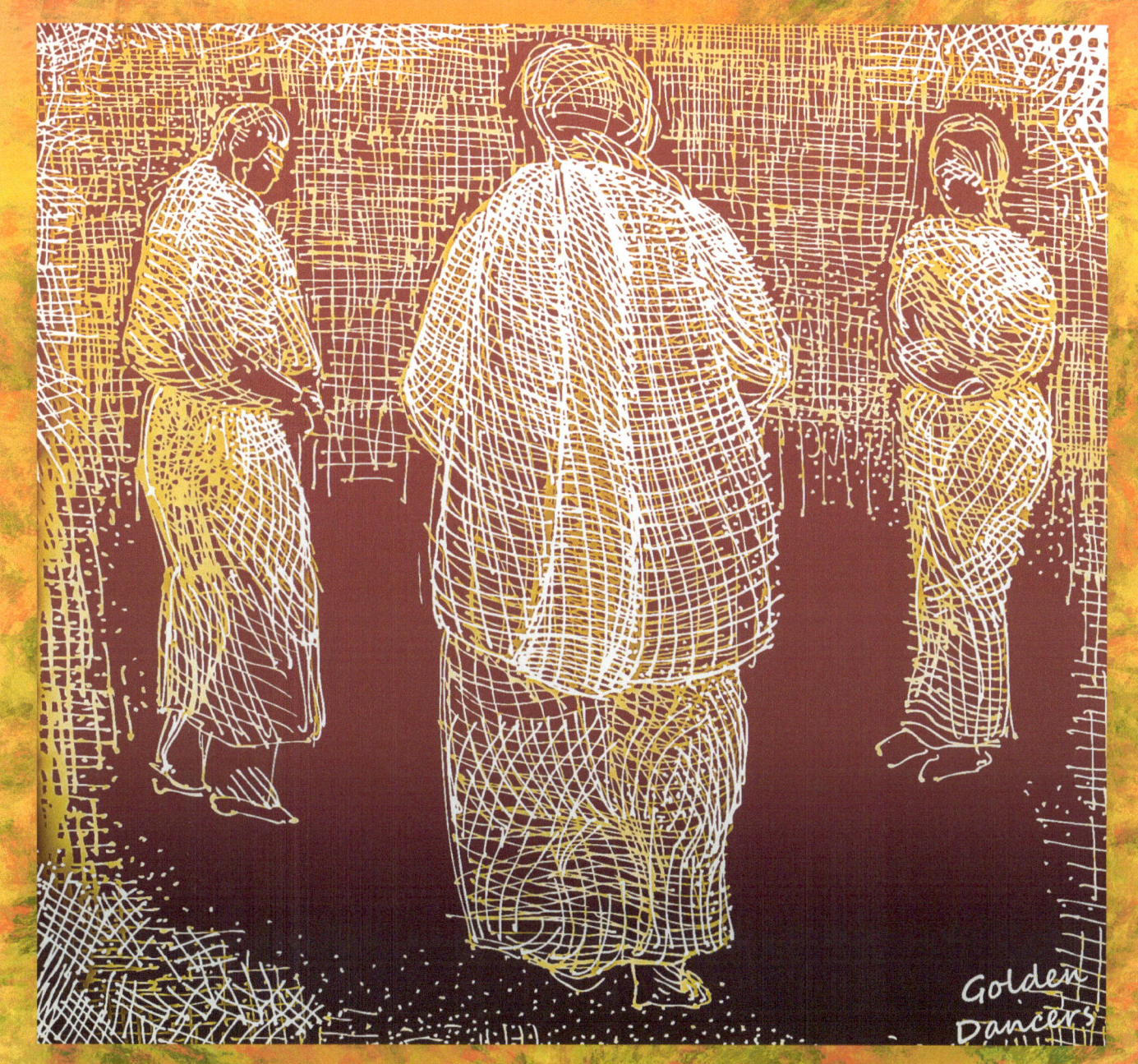

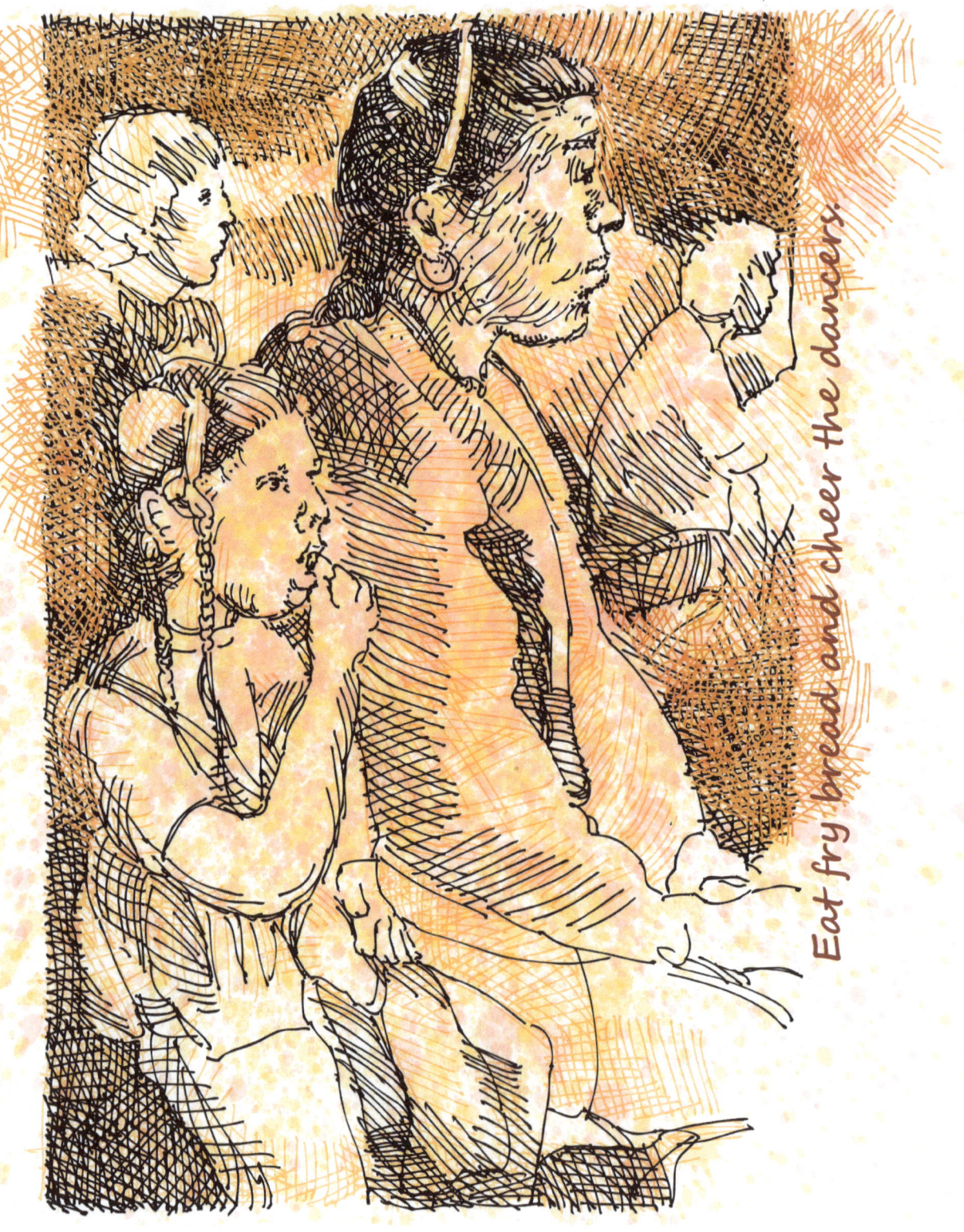

Eat fry bread and cheer the dancers.

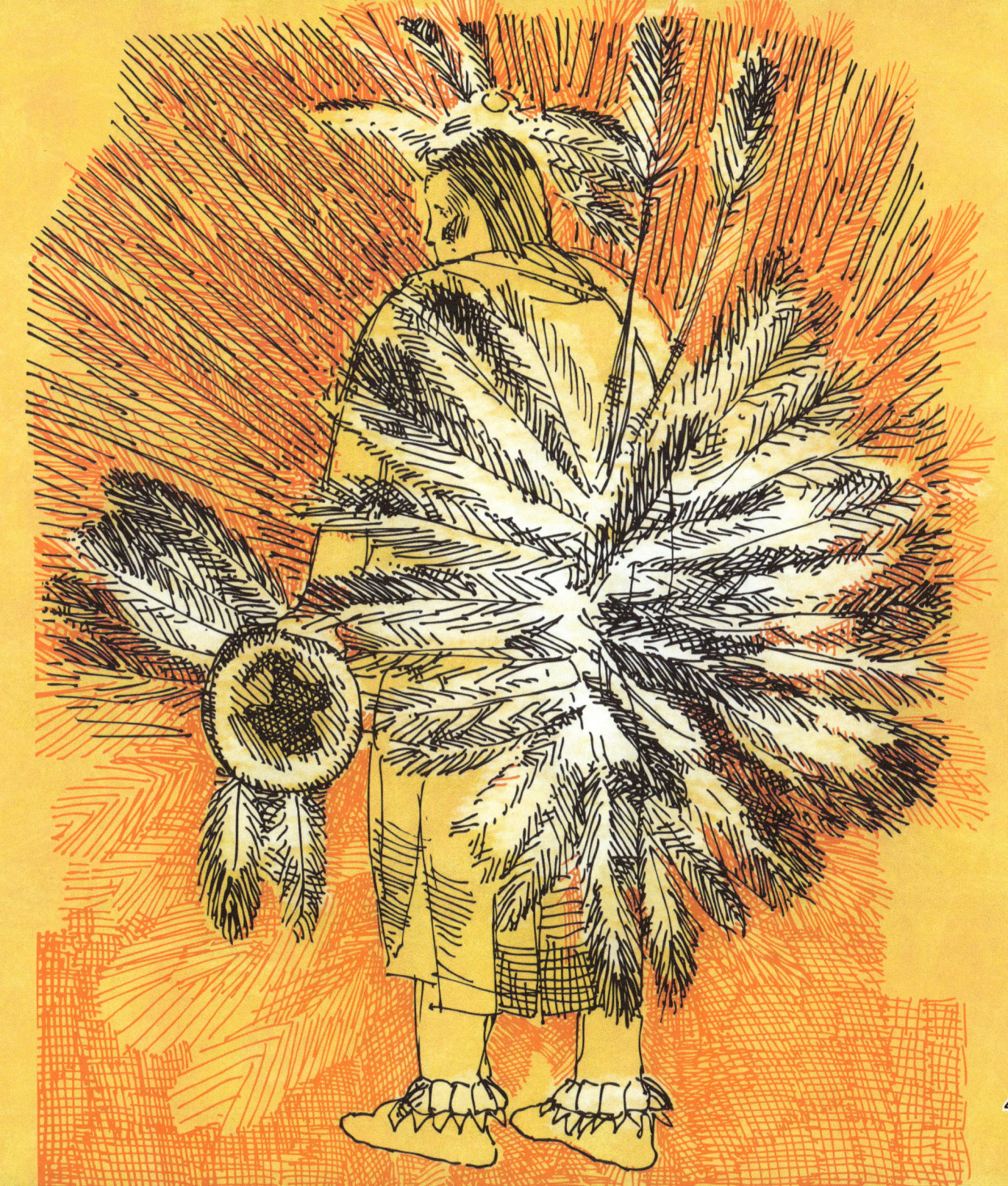

49

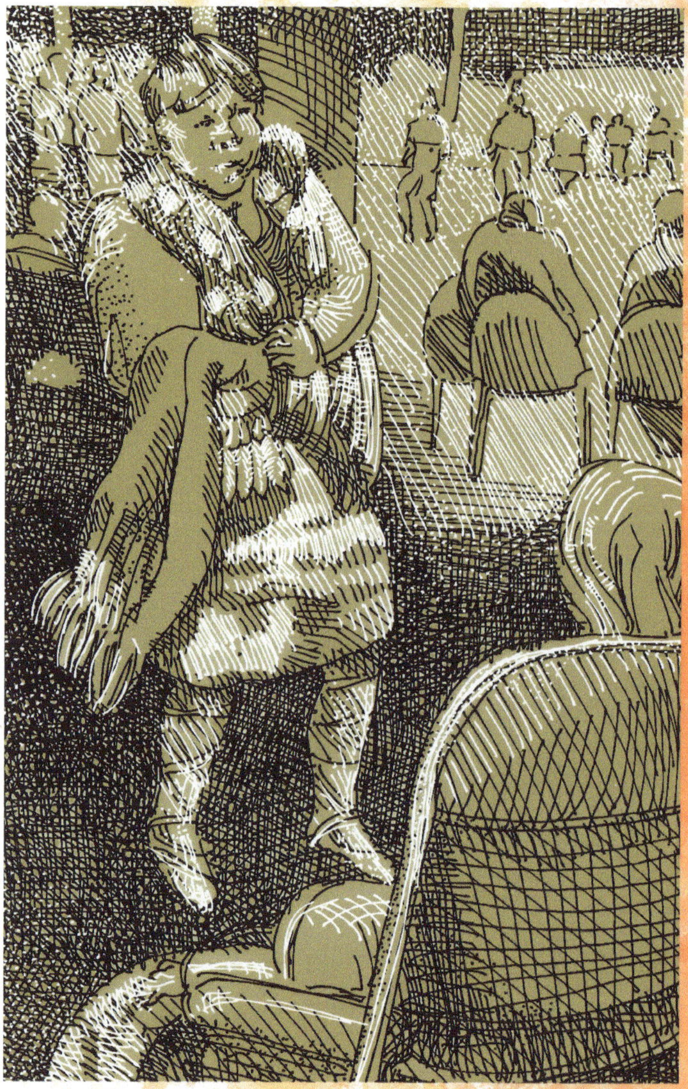

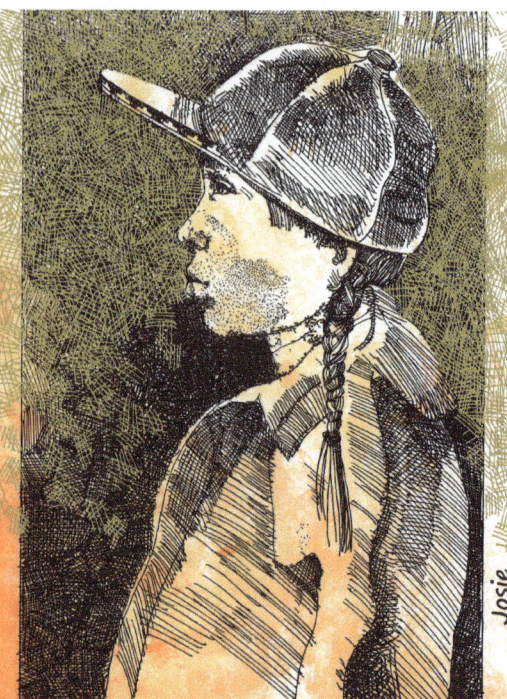

Josie

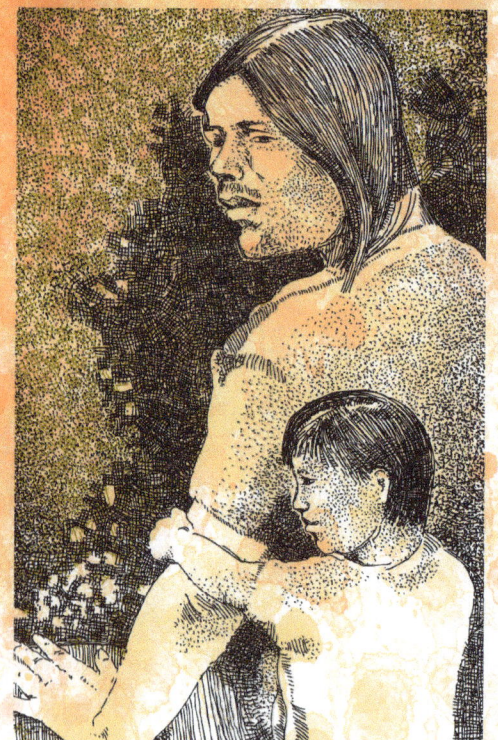

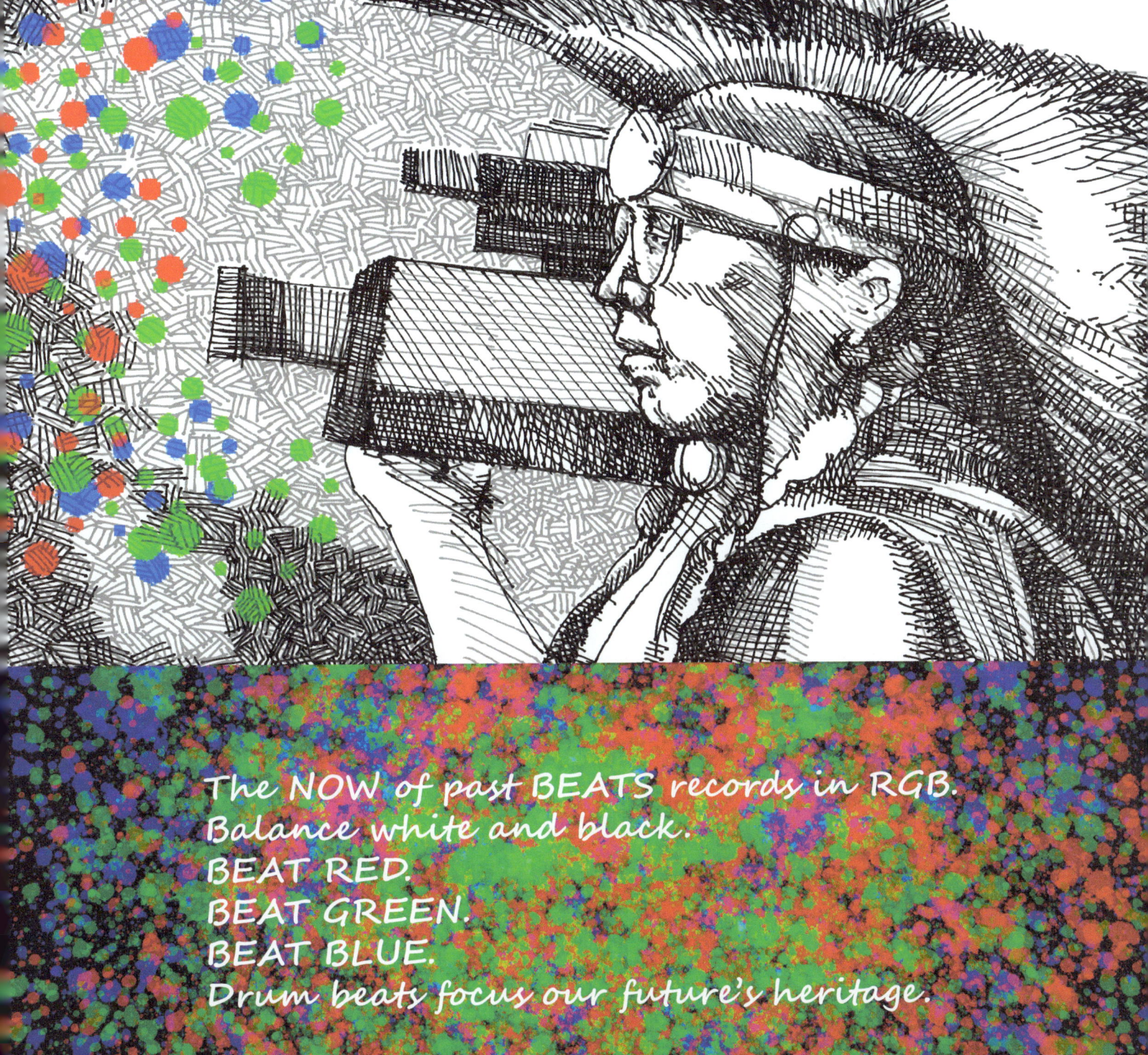

The NOW of past BEATS records in RGB.
Balance white and black.
BEAT RED.
BEAT GREEN.
BEAT BLUE.
Drum beats focus our future's heritage.

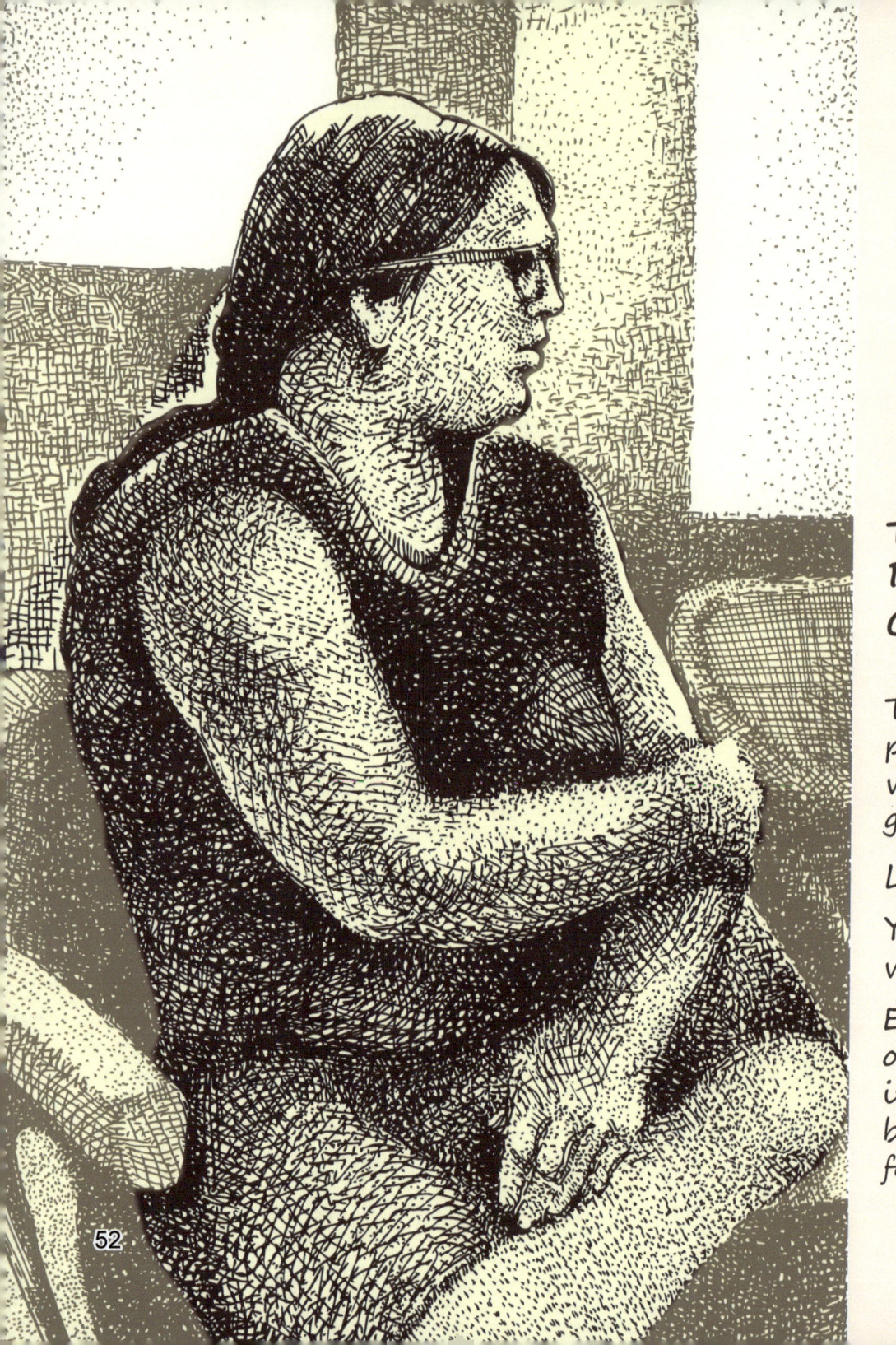

The Chief Redstone Health Center

Through the clear plate glass see the wind blow prairie grass.

Listen to its long notes.

Your appointment waits.

Everyone waited on history and it traded buffalo meat for diabetes.

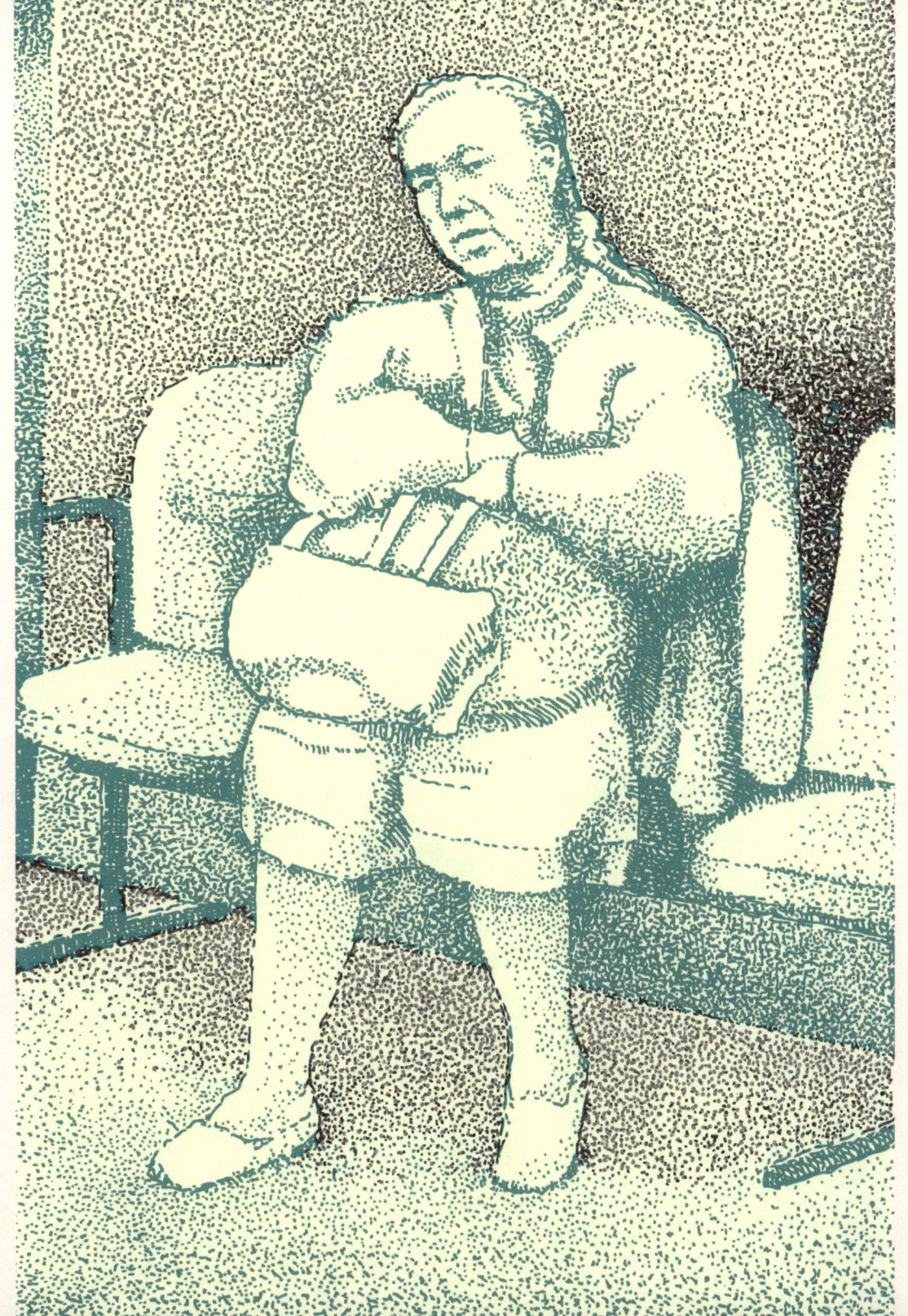

53

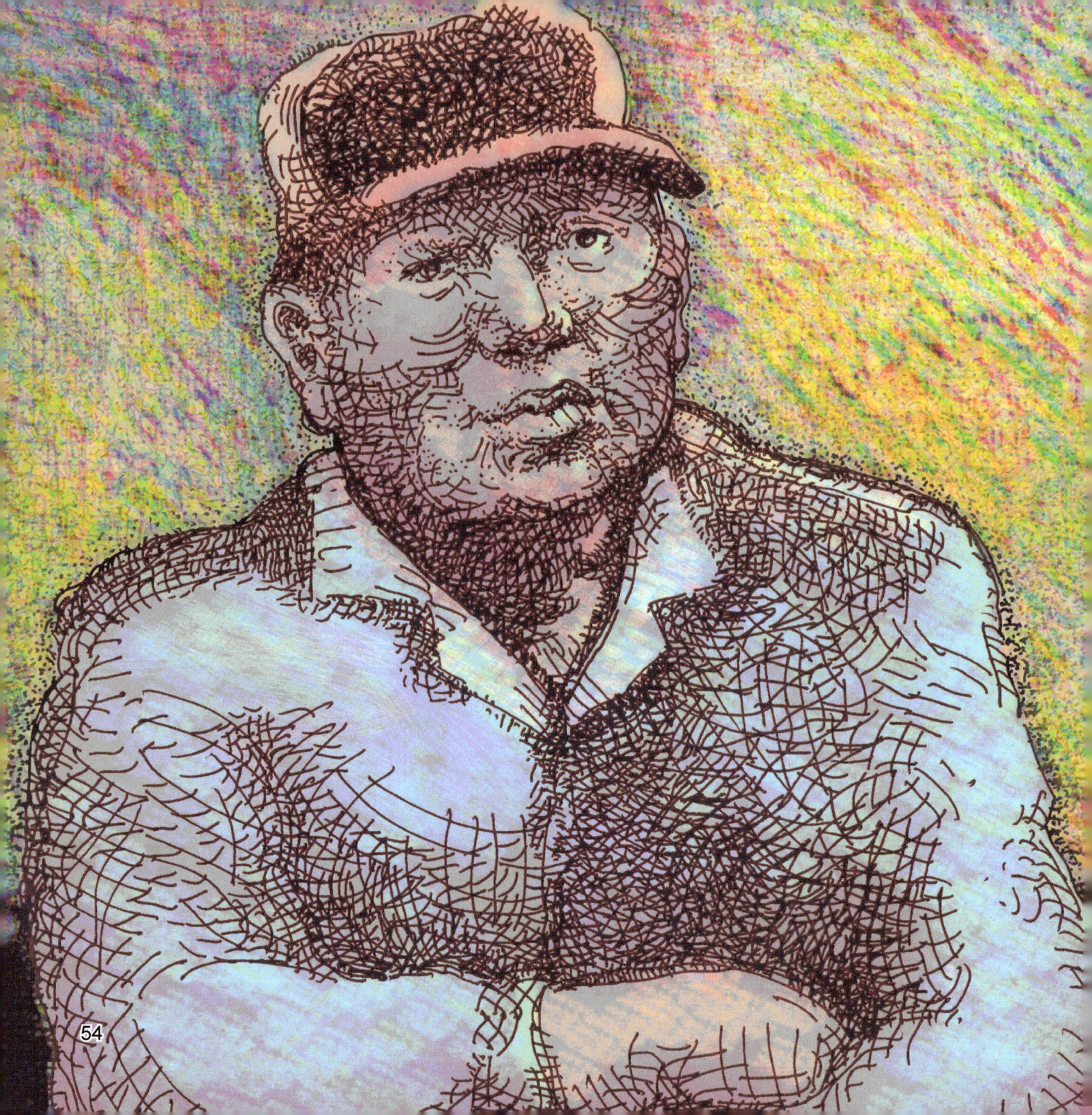

Leslie Fourstar

He watched in silence, alert as a rabbit. Outside the spotless office plate glass the green grass whipped silently. Finally he spoke, "Are you an artist? They say Indians make good artists, but me, I can't even draw a horse."

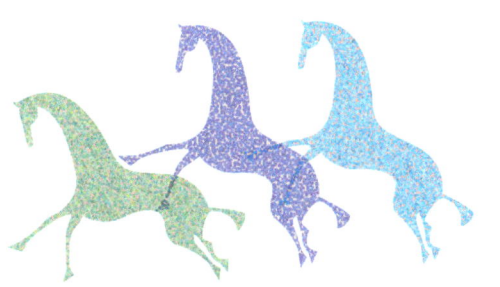

Leslie Fourstar began to speak now with the quiet authority of age. He was the oldest Nakotan elder, descended from the Nakotan chief who had met Lewis and Clark on the Missouri River just a few miles from the Chief Redstone Health Center where we sat.

The nurse appeared, placed her hands, palms down, against a dark navy waiting chair, and leaned her stocky frame forward. "Almost time for the doctor to see you, Leslie; then you can eat. Ham and eggs." Everybody grinned. The talk turned to steak; diabetic tongues watered. My mouth watered. The four seated around me knew the most they could hope for from cattle was skimmed milk.

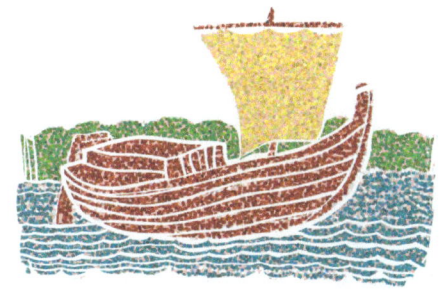

Disease, Leslie continued; his grandfather, at age five, had lost his brother – smallpox in 1837. It was brought as a gift in blankets. The traders said not to open them until after they left. In 1860 a steamship had sunk in the Missouri River; that's when his grandmother was born.

"Let me see." I showed Leslie Fourstar the drawing. He nodded. "I was a lawyer – won twenty-five million dollars' worth of claims against the U.S. government."

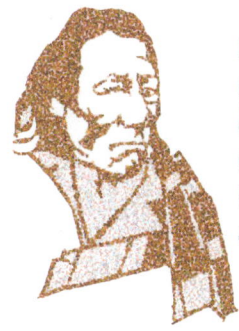

He sifted through subjects, a person reliving his life, reaching out for me, and knowing there was little time between the business of being sick. Chief Big Bear was a relative. He was a war chief during the Riel Rebellion. I imagined French Canadians and Leslie's people being overrun by red Mounties.

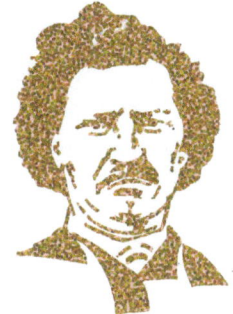

What could I say?

He said it with pride. "On the Fourth of July our veterans marched." He explained: World War II, Korea, Vietnam, and Desert Storm, they carried the President's Flag."

The nurse interrupted, "Leslie?"

When I was a boy my grandfather would raise his stiff old diabetic frame to walk starch legged, his weathered shoes stamping his gray trousers at every step. Leslie headed in to hear the doctor.

I waited. After the doctor's time, he came to me on his way to eat breakfast. I stood to shake his hand.

"The next time you see me, I'm going to be a billion and a half dollar man."

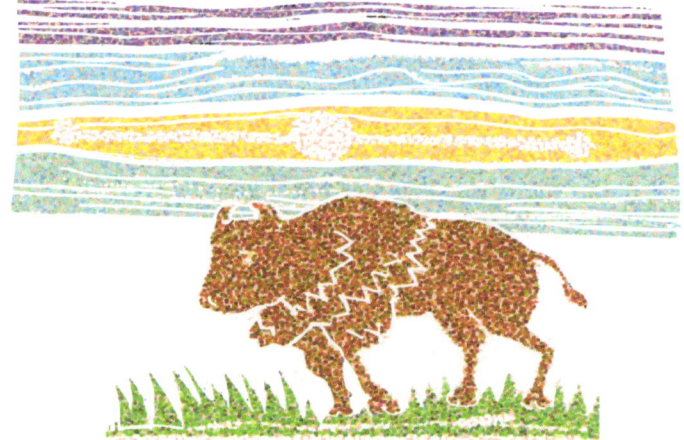

For the first time I felt puzzled.

"Yes," he said, with the confidence of someone who never thinks of lying, and so never thinks he will be disbelieved. Indeed, it was a settlement. An oil and gas settlement with Alberta and Saskatchewan.

I wondered silently what he would do with 1.5 billion dollars.

He raised both hands in communion and announced, "I am going to set up a buffalo herd, and then I will give the rest away." Leslie gave the contented smile of a man who had just ingested a big prime rib. He turned and stiffly walked to the dining room to eat his skimmed milk and cereal.

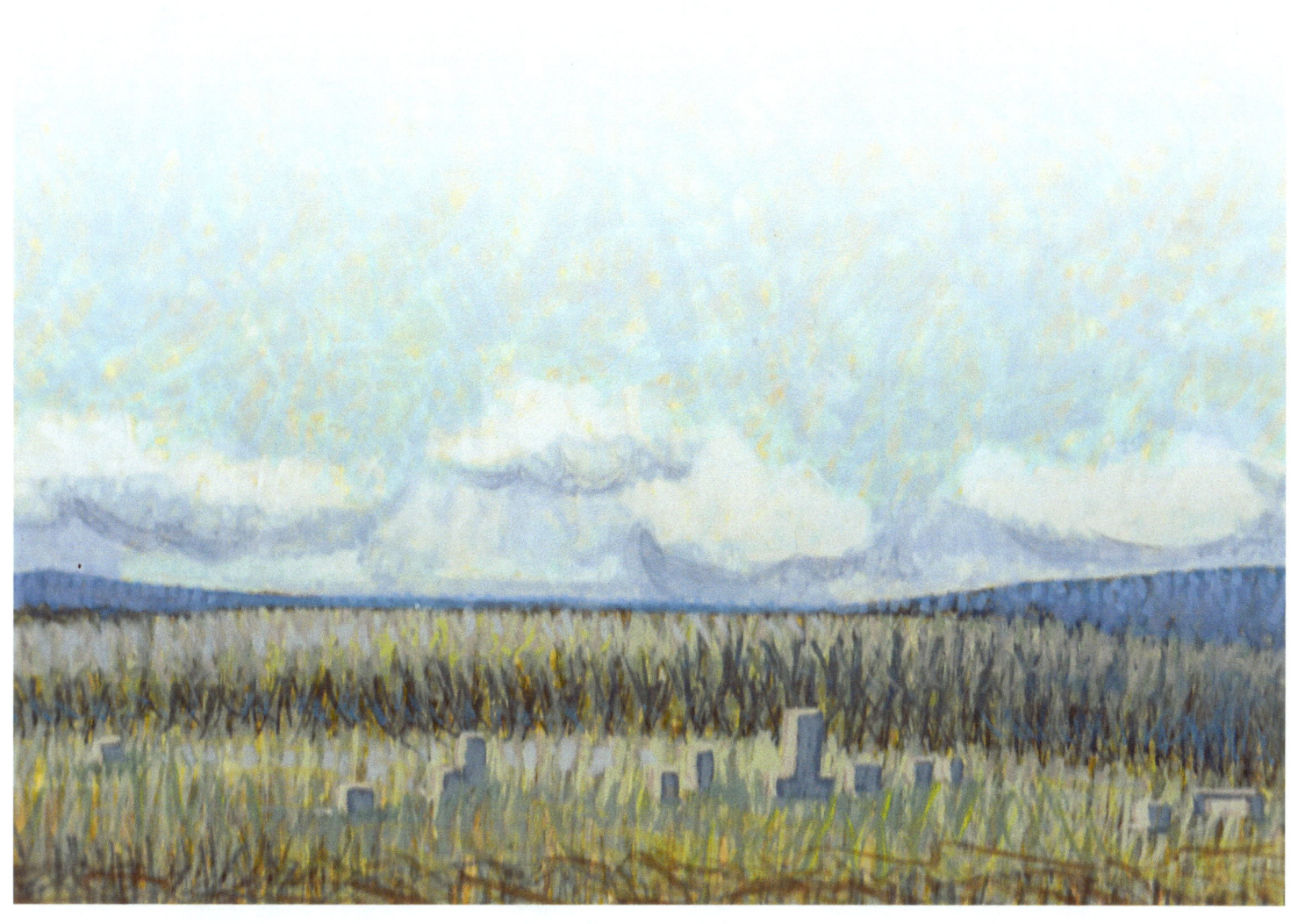

Assiniboine army scout burial grounds

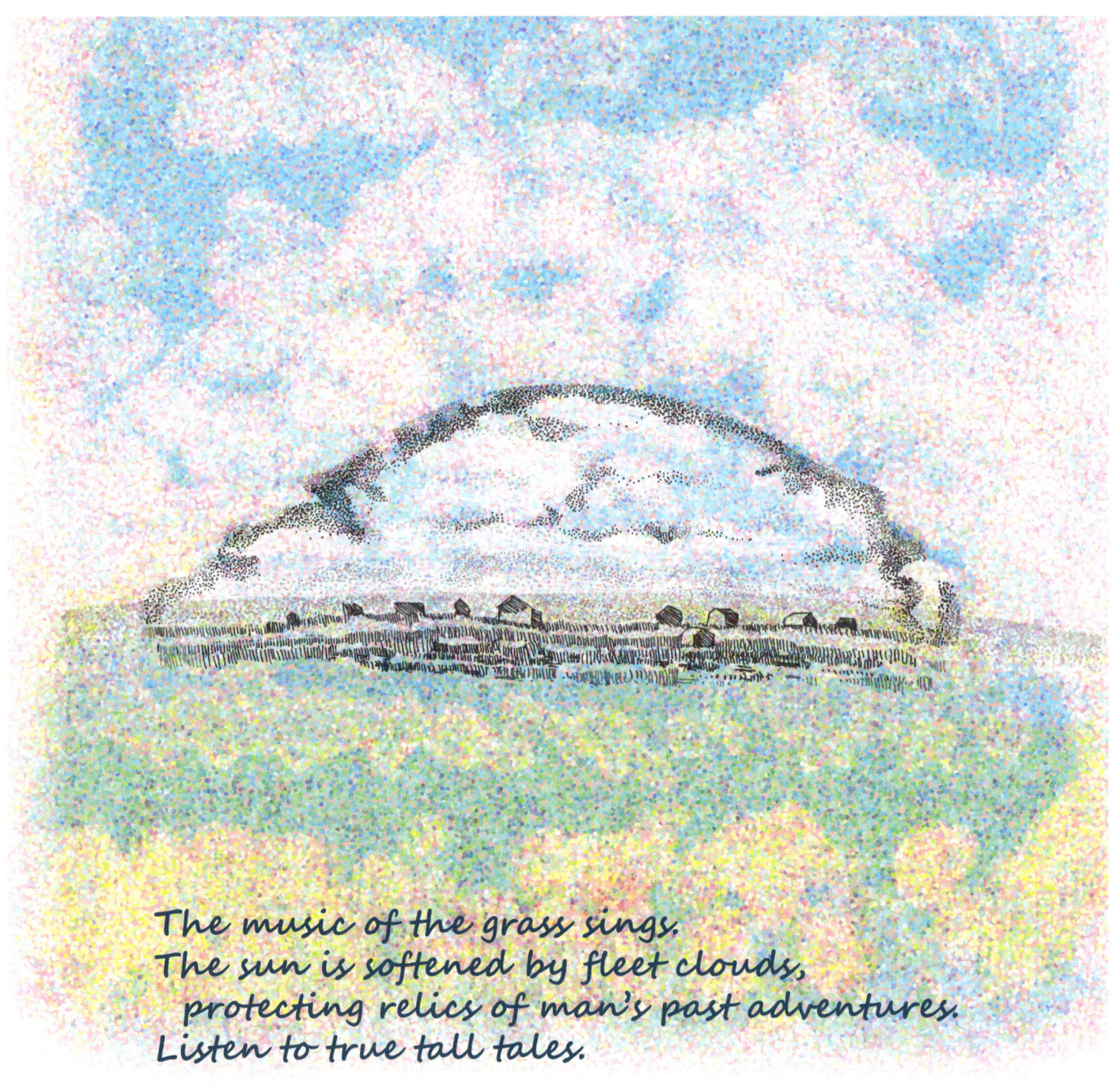

The music of the grass sings.
The sun is softened by fleet clouds,
   protecting relics of man's past adventures.
Listen to true tall tales.

58

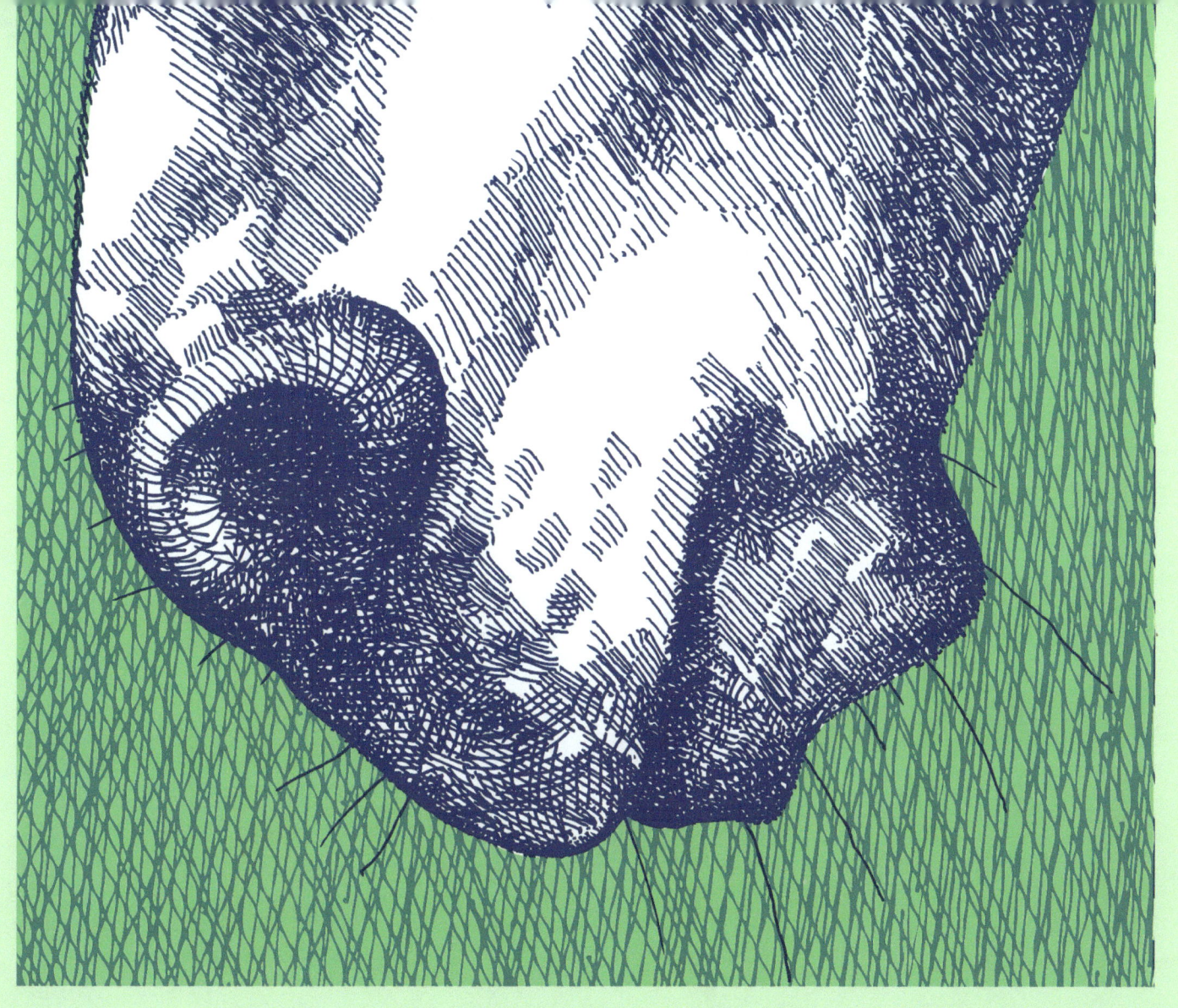

Smell the
sweet odor of grass.

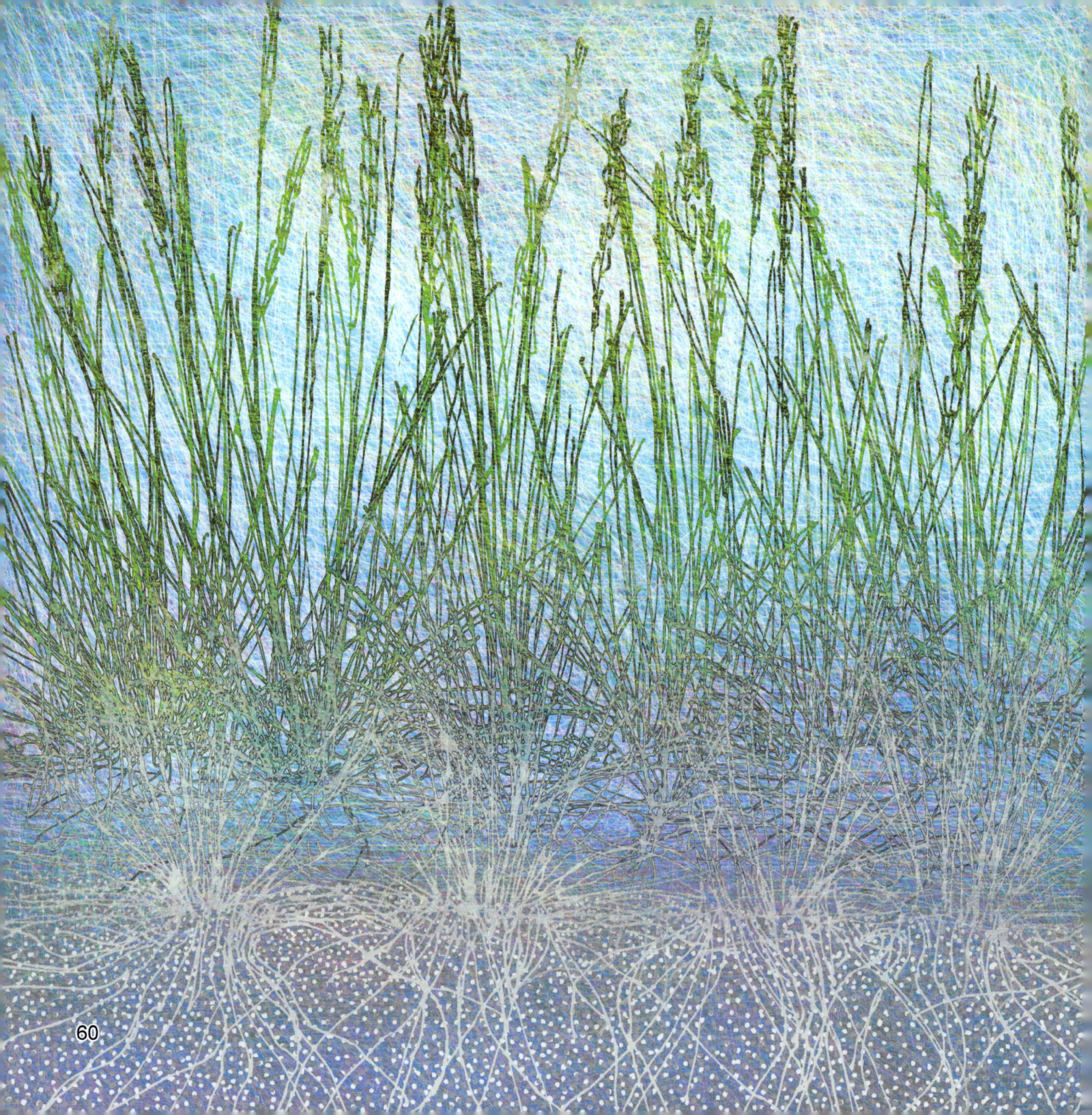

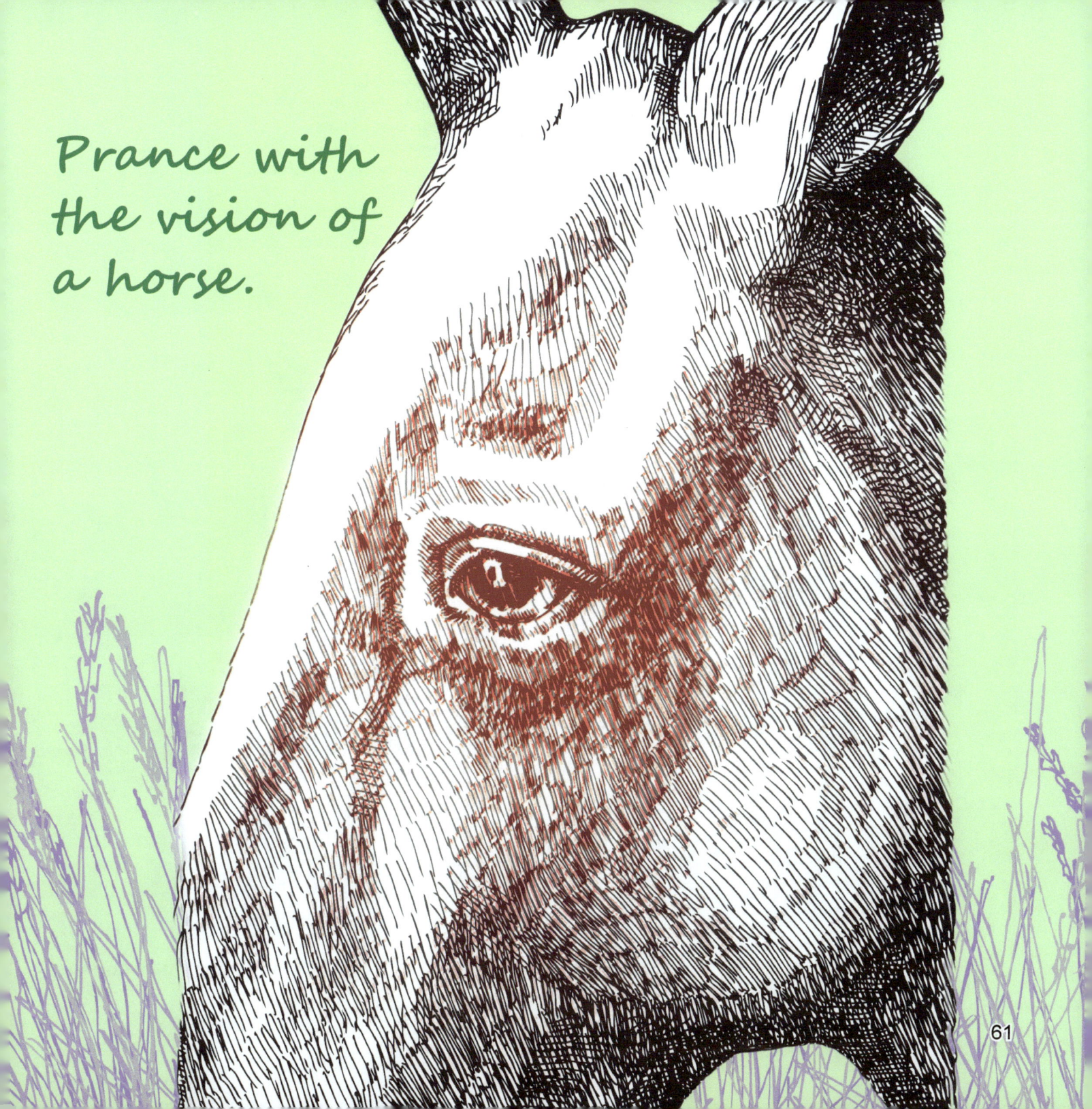

Prance with
the vision of
a horse.

61

Right eye vision includes frontal 65° binocular vision. Monocular side vision extends to the buttock.

Left eye vision includes frontal 65° binocular vision. Monocular side vision extends to the buttock.

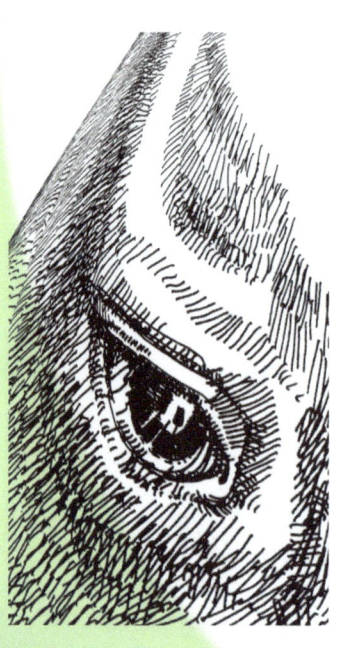

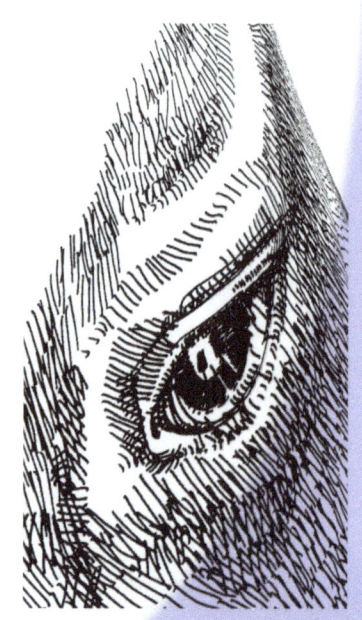

Just like a horse in motion we see the everlasting change within our ARC of GRASS.

Right monocular vision

Binocular vision controlled by head's direction

Left monocular vision

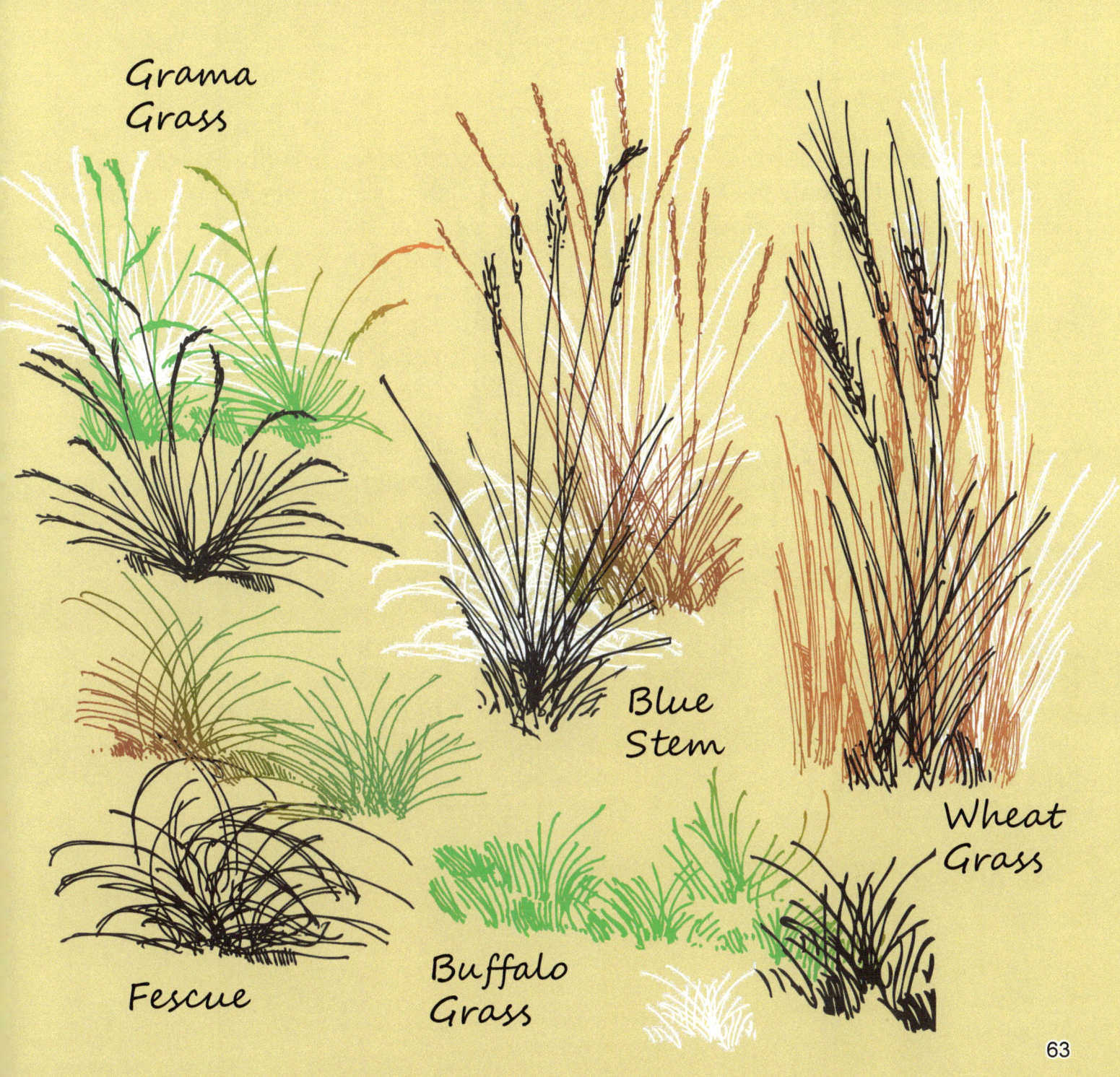

Grama
Grass

Blue
Stem

Wheat
Grass

Fescue

Buffalo
Grass

63

Postfix

My first memory of nature is looking up as a toddler in Wills Point, Texas, at Johnson grass whipping back and forth in the spring breeze. As a young man I was still overwhelmed with the grandeur of grass while living in Glasglow, Montana. In the summer of 1992 I was compelled by this memory to return for a short visit. My Amtrak ticket went as far as Wolf Point. A few years ago I discovered a box of drawings I completed during that trip. I inked them, and new technology permitted me to present them in a manner which developed my thoughts on this environment of grass.

Grasslands present themselves all over the earth: the American Great Plains, the Asian steppes, the pampas of South America and the grasslands of Africa. Wherever a man stands on these endless landscapes, he is confronted with the simple truth that it is a land and landscape that, like the ocean, cannot be measured. When one stands in the middle of prairie grass one knows the earth is round, but there is no means to calibrate what one sees: no mountain, no trees, no building. How does one know his own size? Are we big or small? What does time mean in an endless space? It leaves us in awe. We can not live in perpetual awe, and so we say that the great prairies are boring, that they are "drive through" or "fly over" country. The animals and people that live on these endless spaces accept and love them. They are what they are.

They are awe filled.

Glen Smith
Normangee, Texas
2015

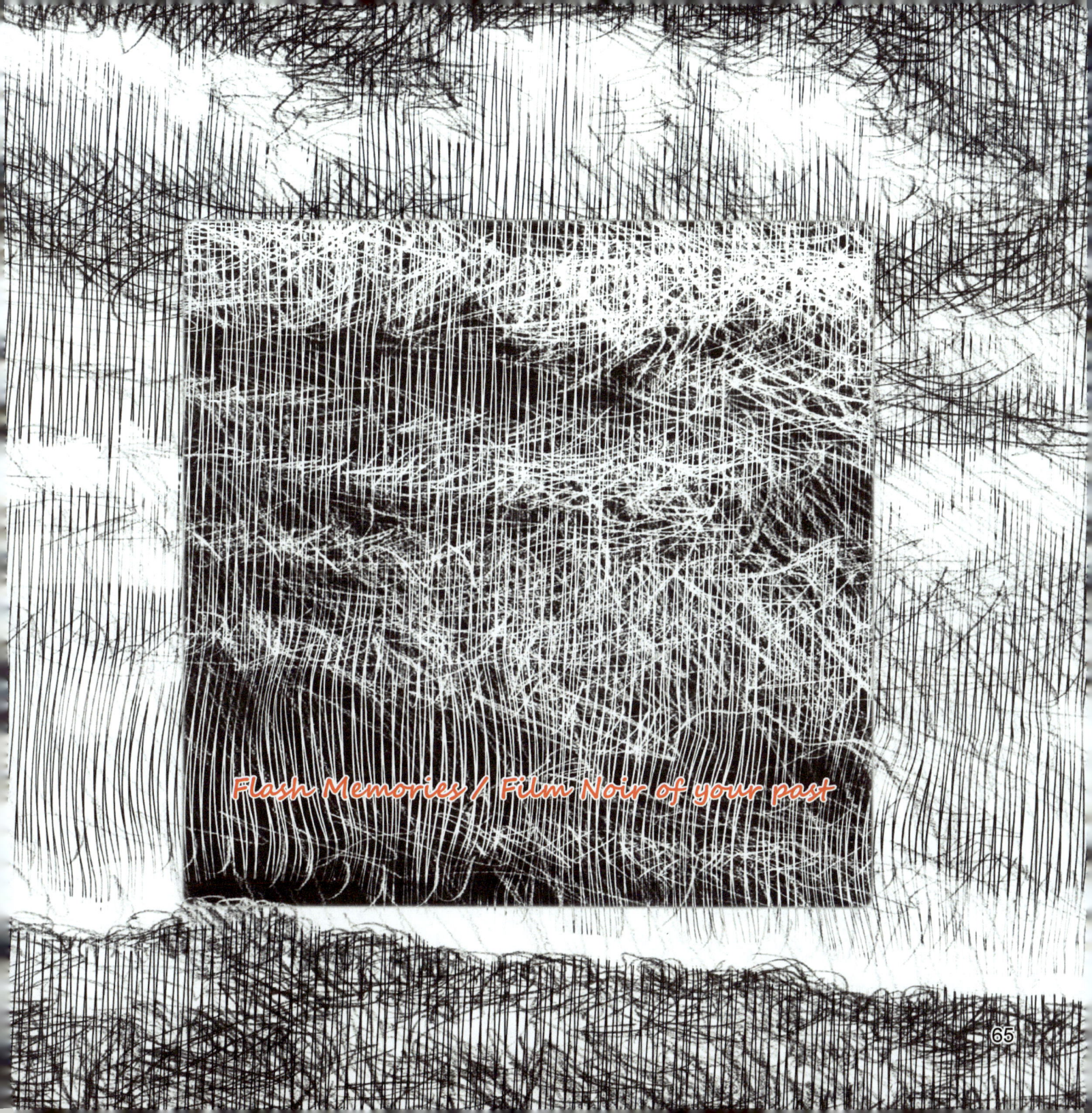

Flash Memories / Film Noir of your past

65

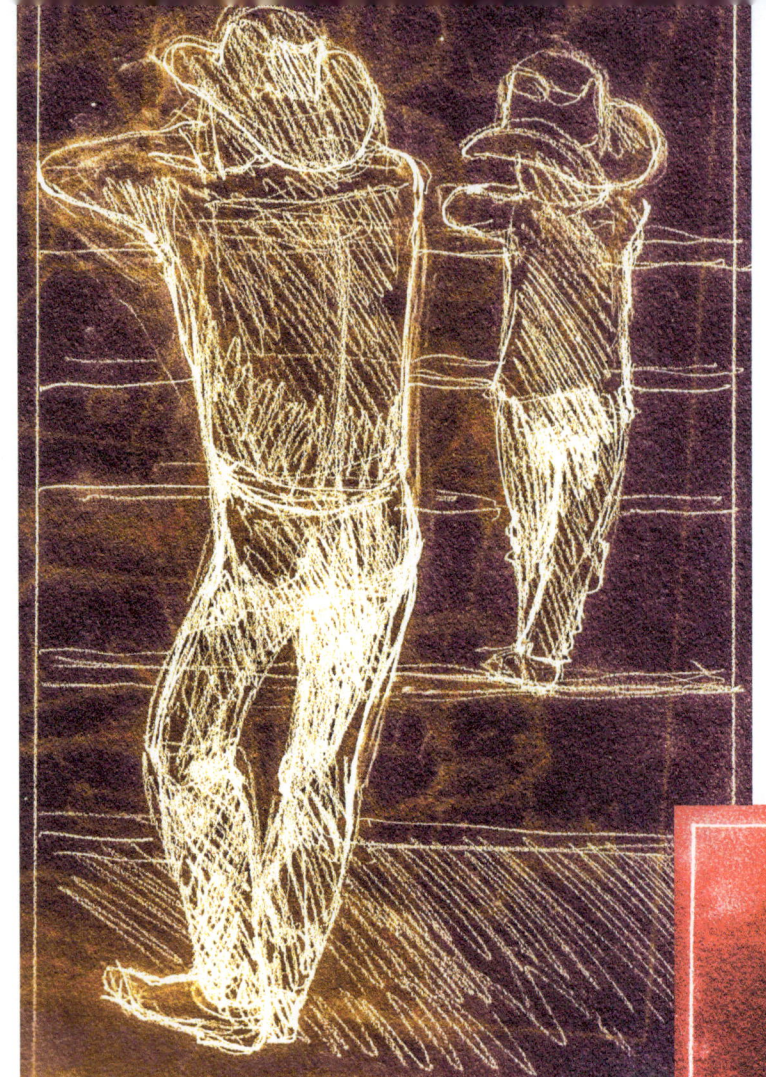

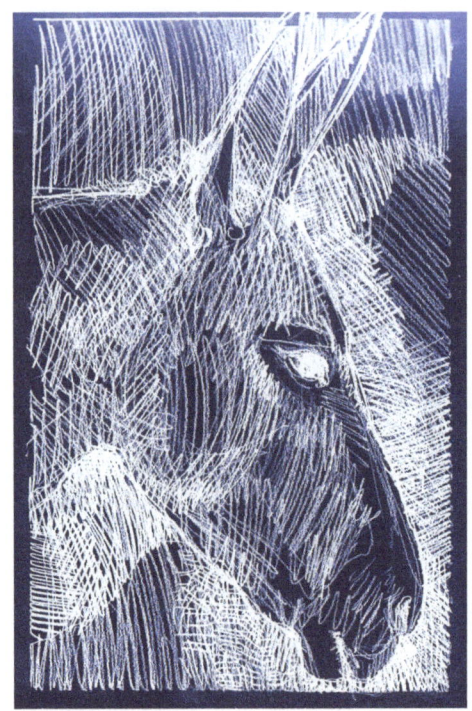

Sudden raw memories
without context
may not lead to
understanding.

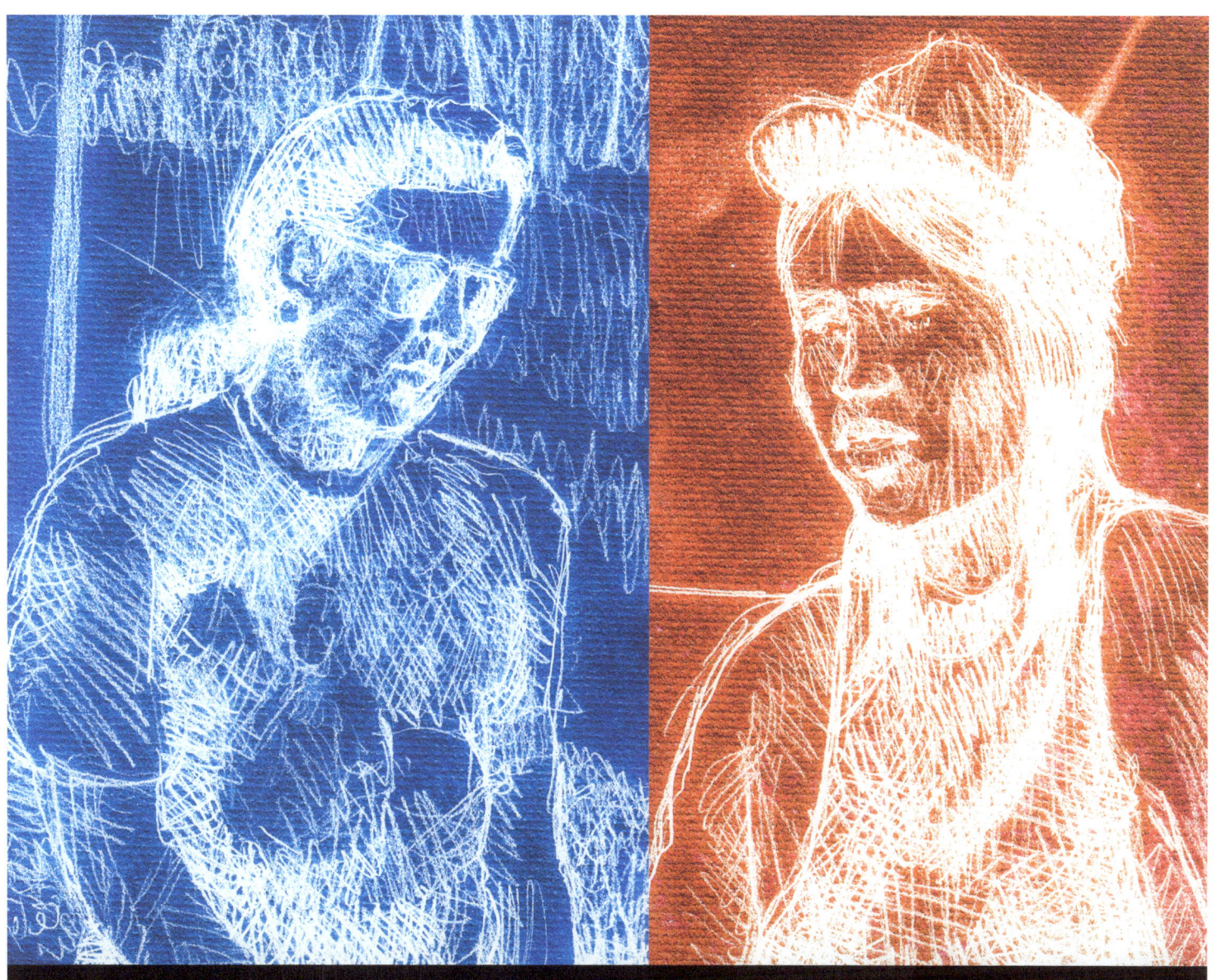

They may recreate remembered feelings.

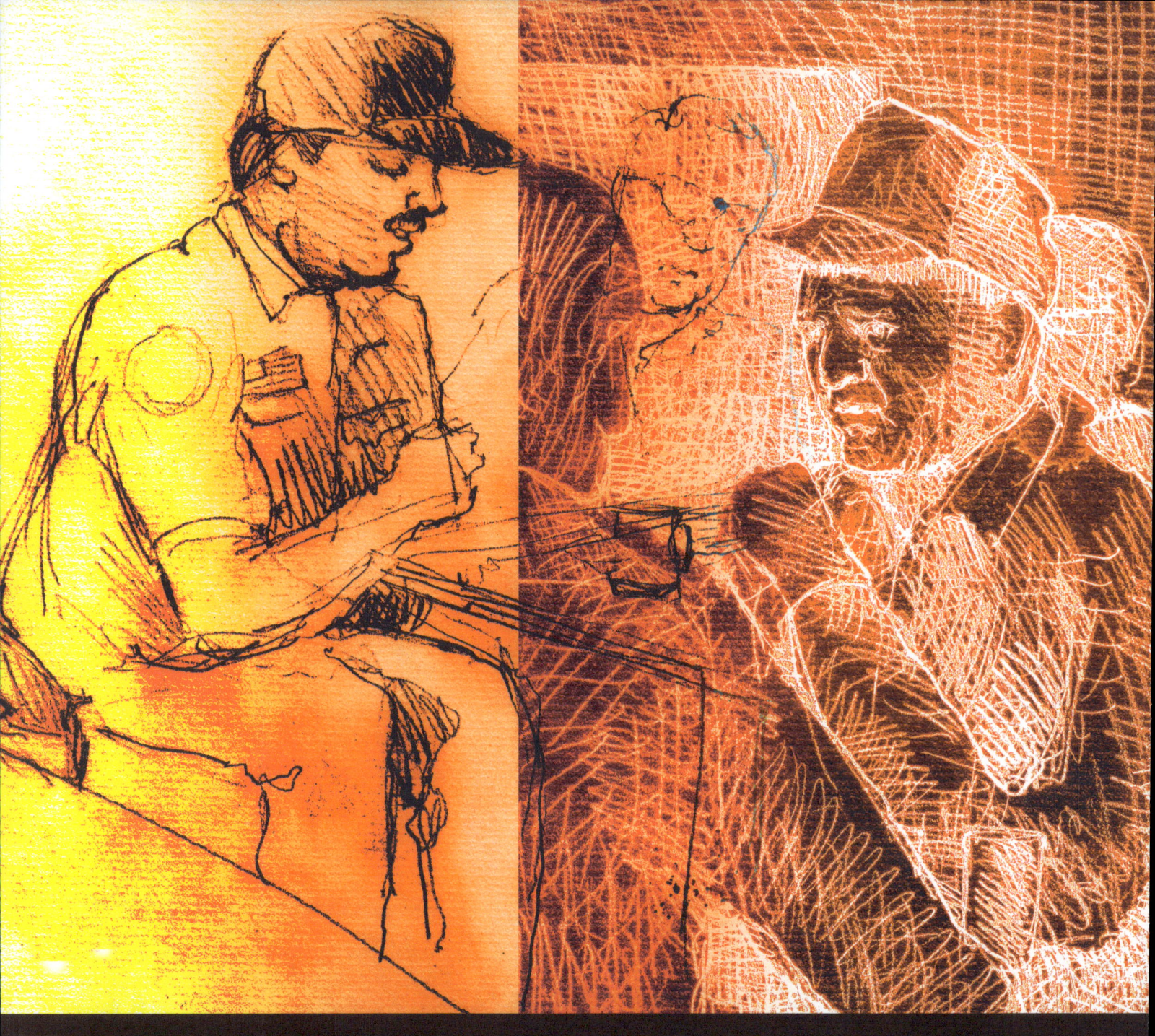

Sound memories jumble.

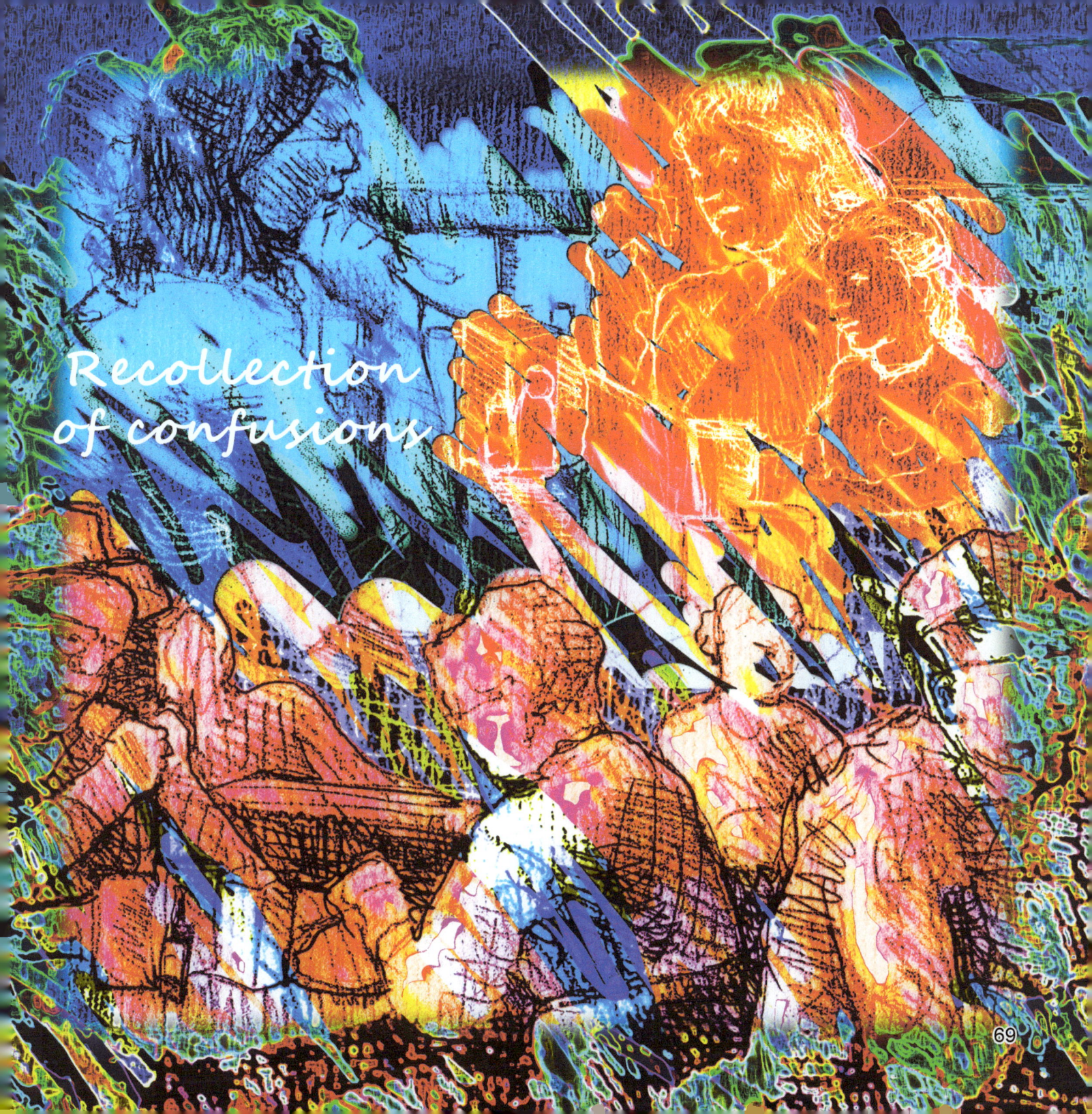

Recollection
of confusions

69

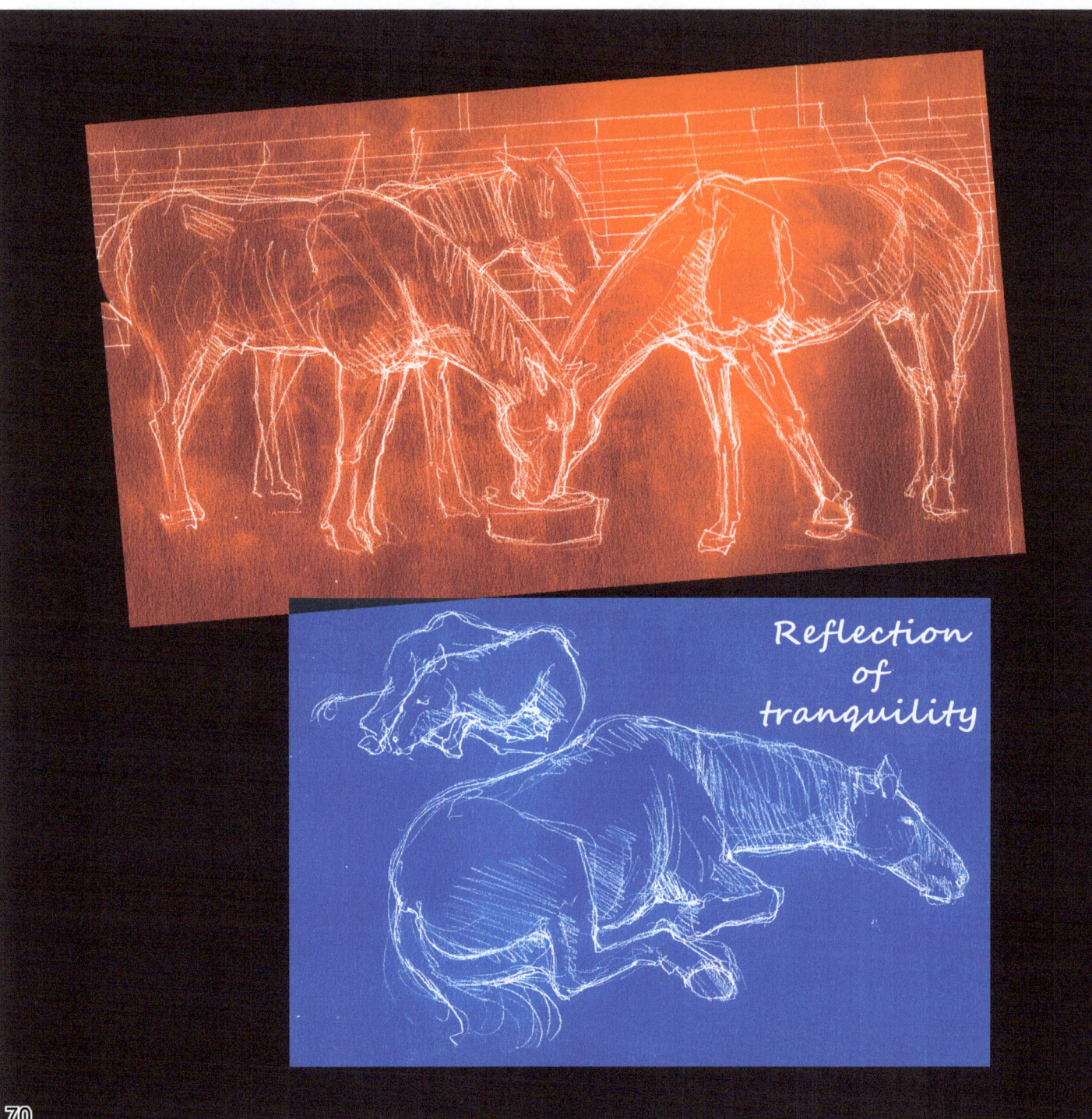

Reflection
of
tranquility

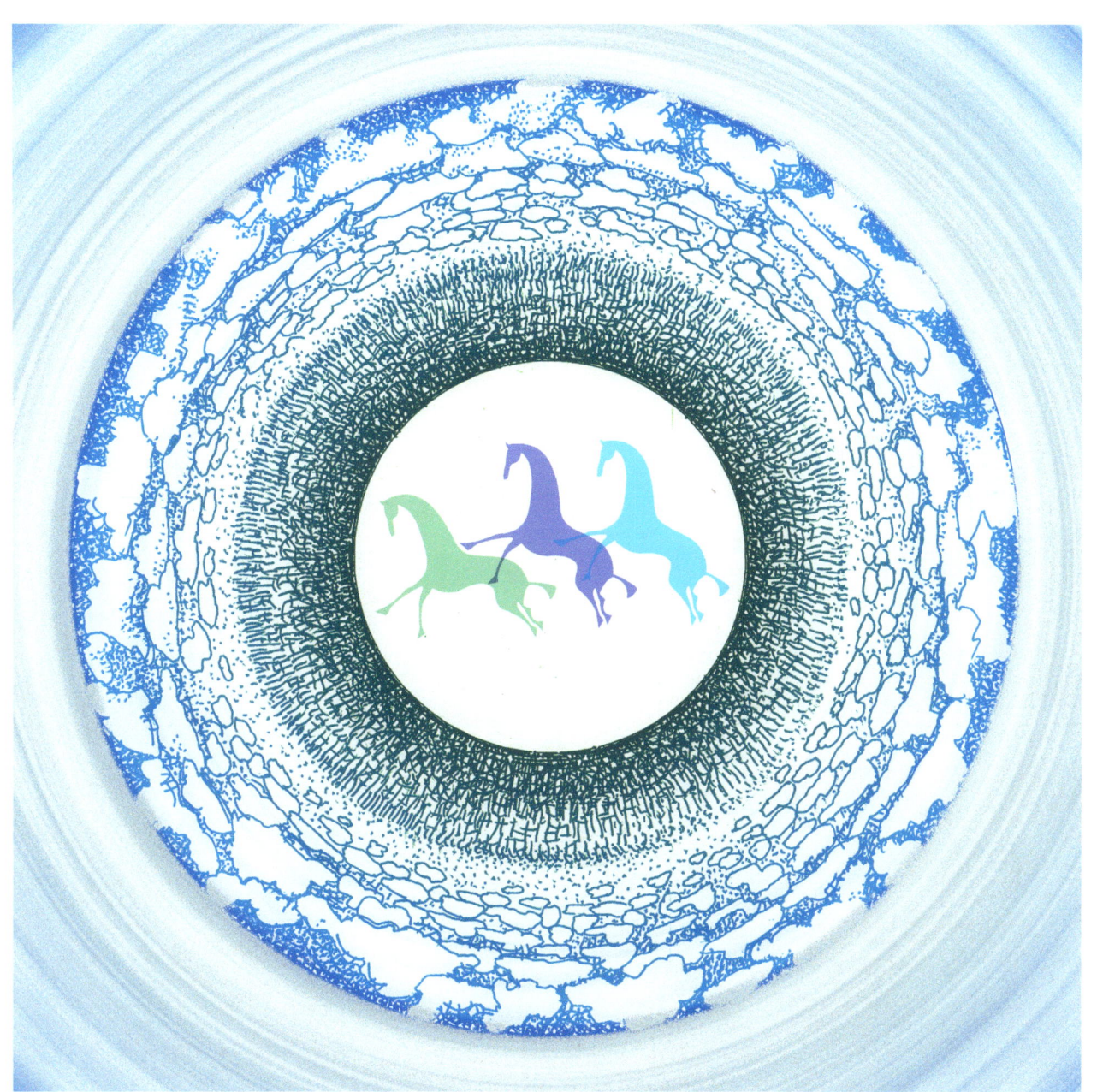

On our rolling prairie we can image an Earth covered with grass. We then roam with our free will like wild mustangs. Yet we are men.

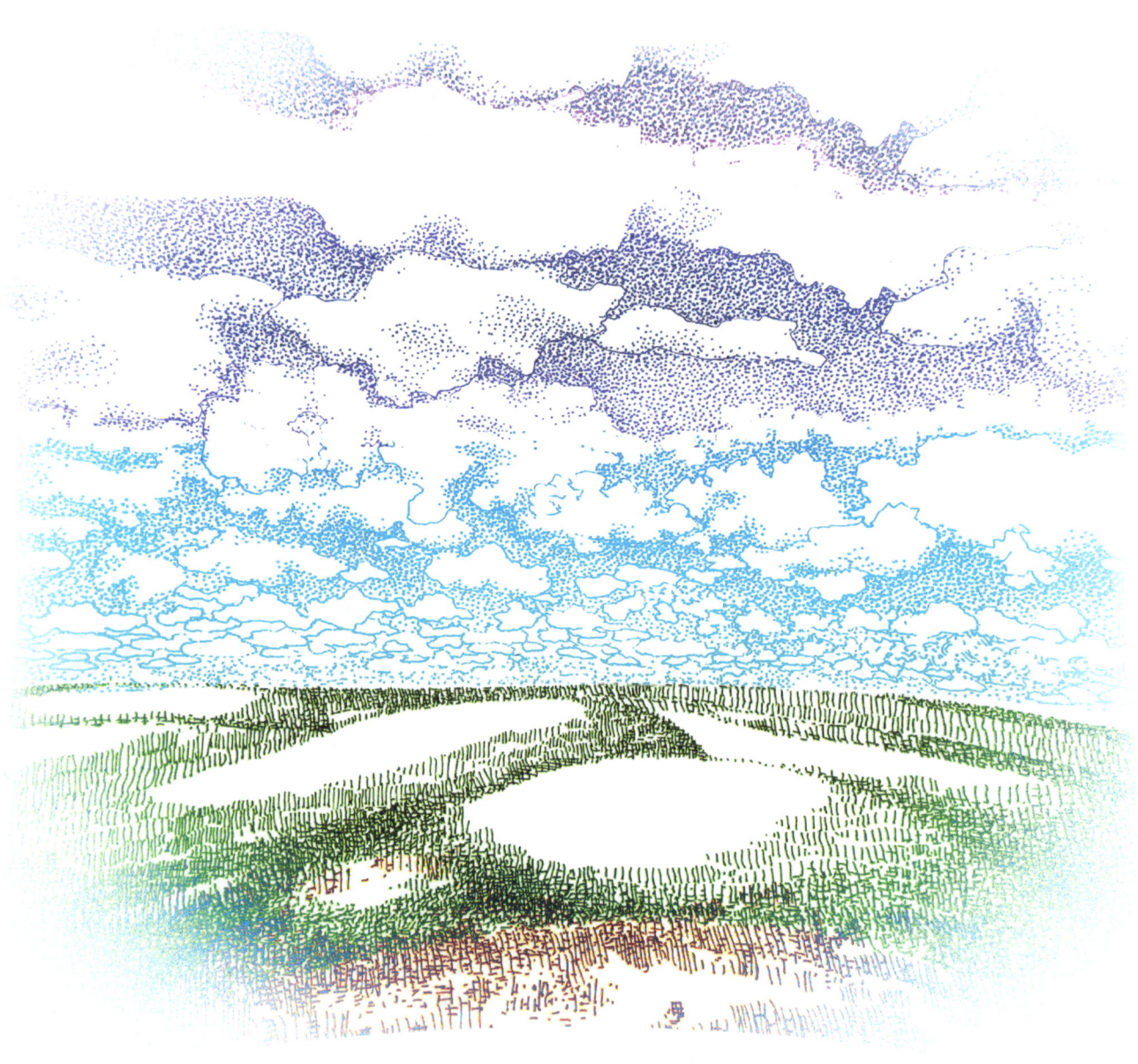

www.ingramcontent.com/pod-product-compliance
Lightning Source LLC
Chambersburg PA
CBHW050854180526
45159CB00007B/2675